CRACK

Also by Joy Howard

SECOND BITE
(with Hilary J Murray and Gina Shaw)

A TWIST OF MALICE (ed)

EXIT MOONSHINE

CRACKING ON

*Poems on Ageing by
Older Women*

Edited by Joy Howard

First published in 2009 by Grey Hen Press
PO Box 450
Keighley
West Yorkshire
BD22 9WS
www.greyhenpress.com

ISBN 978-0-9552952-4-9

Printed 2009
Reprinted 2010

Printed by: Winstonmead Print, Loughborough,
Leicestershire LE11 1LE

With thanks to all the contributors for their fearlessness in facing the looking-glass, and finding beauty in telling the truth.

In a dream you are never eighty.

Anne Sexton

Age seldom arrives smoothly or quickly. It's more often a succession of jerks.

Jean Rhys

Old age ain't no place for sissies.

Bette Davis

Preface

All the contributors to this anthology are over sixty – many have reached an even more distinguished age. We have experienced loss: of parents, of partners, of faculties. Some of us are living with chronic illness. All of us have come to the time of life when death has to be confronted.

There are sources of joy too that only come with age: grandchildren, freedom from the daily grind, giving two fingers to keeping up appearances, the endurance and sometimes unexpectedness of love.

In this book you will find plenty of examples of courage, wit, self-knowledge, a spirited engagement with life and an acceptance of both sides of the balance sheet. Collecting these poems has been a source of inspiration and delight.

Joy Howard

Contents

Mind the Gap

Sick and Tired

Good Loving

Letting Go

The Missing

Nearly There?

Departure Lounge

Coda

Biographical Notes

Index of Poets

Acknowledgments

Foreword

It wasn't until I reached my fifties and had my eighty-nine year old mother to stay that I realised I was called an old woman, lumped into the same category as my mother. We were both in the second half of our lives and on the way downhill, to death or the scrap-heap. At least that's what younger people thought. How could I be in the same age group as my mother? But I was, because everyone over sixty is called old. To the young, that means an unattractive, decrepit, incapacitated, possibly demented, empty husk of a person. They seem to be frightened of us because they think we're a useless burden coming their way, which is only going to get heavier and drain them of all their time, strength and money.

But they're quite wrong, of course, which is why they need these poems as much as we do, to show them what being an older woman is really like. Beginning to read these poems, I began to cry at the very first line, cried all through the Orphaned section, and on through the Grandmothers, because the poems punch you in the heart. There are your deepest feelings, loves and fears in front of you on the page. There is a reflection of some large or small part of yourself in every poem. But there is nothing miserable or timid about them. They are full of life, bursting with it, even when they speak of death and loss, and they are not about the end of life. They are about whole lives, about real old age, which is full of wisdom, experience, pain, happiness, wit, excitement, discovery, memories – everything that every age experiences.

I am not a poet, I write prose, usually humorous, because I am perhaps scared of getting too close to the emotions and experiences expressed in these wonderful poems, the softness of a baby skin, and of the touch of much loved and much older skin, the tenderness and closeness, or the distance and spikiness, between generations. Outrage is easier for me, but that is here too, particularly in Mind the Gap, which challenges the young head on, rather than fading out quietly and letting them, and everyone else, continue to believe that youth is everything and old age is nothing much at all. Unrepentant, unapologetic, brave, confident and beautiful, these poems show that we older women deserve to live as full and rich a life as any other generation. And the nearer we get to the end, through Sick and Tired, Nearly There and into the Departure Lounge, the braver we get. Or at least these poets do. For those of us who are scared stiff, then these poems can help us through it.

Michele Hanson

Prelude

Last Haiku

No, wait a minute,
I can't be old already:
I'm just about to

Connie Bensley

1

Orphaned

Forecast
for my father

I'd not have known you in your dimming light,
the way that shadows shrunk your breath
until it slipped its mooring with you in tow.

They said those last few days
had pared you down – as fast
as tapering a candle to fit the candlestick.

You disappeared into the night
just ten minutes
before your wall clock chimed the hour.

My radio, a hundred miles away,
prepared to circumnavigate
Low Faroes, Viking, FitzRoy.

Then, *A Vigorous Low, Severe Gale 9,*
Violent Storm 11. Somehow I knew
not to call the coastguard.

A corona of automatic beams
sweep round from the land's vague edge.
Somewhere, a candle guttering.

That completes the Shipping Forecast
a voice says, before, *Wishing you*
a very good night. And then the pips.

Pat Borthwick

5

To My Parents

how could you

I have my family to care for
and I'm jogging along okay
when you begin to go downhill

then just as my daughter starts
to become a woman and my son
moves from junior to senior
one after the other you two
choose to depart this life
without so much as a by your leave

how could you

what am I supposed to do now
whose feet do I lay their little triumphs at
who do I mock-moan about them to
who's going to point out which of our ancestors
they got their tics and quirks and mannerisms from
or which virtues I can claim for our side

where can I go and flop back into my place
which has been kept warm for me
and know I don't have to try to be somebody
or to be the one who makes the rules
where will I go home to now to have my bottle filled

how could you leave me like this
I'm not old enough to be the older generation
and surely you must know at my age
I'm much too old to be left an orphan

Gina Shaw

6

Remains
for my father

Not much: shoes, a tartan dressing-gown,
your tools in order, oiled and silent
in their slender drawers.

Be done by nightfall, I thought,
clutching my sheaf of black bags –

don't remember nightfall –

you'd wrapped it in a yellow cloth
in that careful way of yours –

remember my fingers set solid on its shaft,

that single bullet in its chamber,

the terrifying *what if* thoughts.

Gill McEvoy

Some Midnights

I am from nowhere in particular
nowhere that's on any map
but I go back at certain times
red and blue moons
the winter solstice
some midnights
search for clues in box
after box of torn photographs
tarnished costume jewellery
look for your face in shots
of high-breasted women
uncorseted competent
who smile mysteriously
from under big hats
their hands always folded
hands not unlike my own
that can bake stitch
hold a pencil in private
make it speak for them

and in the crackling air
before the hem of sleep
comes unstitched
I expect you any minute
to step through the arch
of my longing
in a Chanel suit
or a Dior gown
your wrists heavy with bracelets
not unlike the ones
in those boxes

your lips paint-box vermillion
I wait for you to lean down
tattoo my cheek
with their colour whisper
what comes next
when I don't know

Wendy Klein

Lullaby

Once the measured snick
of her mother's needles nudging
each other along the woollen rows
was a metronome for sleep.

Gone, along with wind-up clocks,
the hiss and plop
of gas and Tilley lamp,
the summer nightingale.

Now in the long, long nights the old endure
she lies there, listening for the soothing
slip-tick-tack of someone knitting
her to sleep.

Gill McEvoy

Travelling North
for my mother

It came to me
at Hawick   in the
border country

Doing what I always
do   on holiday
at a pit-stop
head for the shops
a CD   a book a present
for someone

This is a mill town
here is the mill
there are the jumpers
the cashmere   the soft
the pretty   and here am I
with tear-water turning
the heart like an old
mill wheel

I want to buy you
a jumper
and you'll never be glad
of one   of me
again

All week running
in the wild race
of mourning   now sinking

like a stone thrown
into a mill pond

You're gone
and I'm
in another land

Joy Howard

After Dad Died

She became that kid the teacher asked you
to look after, the one you played a trick on,
the one who wore a posh coat and was too scared
to balance along the water-pipe, the one
who didn't see the point of worm-racing,
the one who'd never set foot in a caravan
or owned a rat or lied her way into an A film
or borrowed her sister's nylons and sat
on that bench for a bet to count how many
lorry-drivers gave her a honk. The one
who wouldn't nick three-pence to buy chuddy,
or shout *Where's your boyfriend's shirt?*
at Sylvia with the big bum, too chicken
to test the ice on the dyke or walk barefoot
through the ashes. The one on the edge
of the playground who was dying to go home.

Carole Bromley

All Things Considered

His face was fleshless as a monument – eagle nose sensitive
to lies; lips clenched for whistling or stretched to nothing in a
                                                    smile;
eyebrow-thickets over hazel eyes that peered through pitted
                                                    lenses
at *Ferdinand* every bedtime for a month.

But it's the hands that were my father: welding-scarred with
granite palms; square nails on tufted fingers that could bend
an iron bar to make runners for a sledge, tickle a Triumph back to
                                                    life,
fill a page with writing as even as the thread on a 2-gauge screw.
They smelled of St Bruno Roughcut, gunk and soap; could throw
a ball over the sun; catch and perch a girl on sky-high shoulders;
cool a burning forehead. And when nothing else would settle
bedtime riots, sting a flinching thigh with a single slap
that hurt more than flesh.

On that final day he lay full-length in bed, cat snoring softly
on his legs. I kissed his ironed-out forehead one last time
and carry with me still, the chill of it.

Gill Learner

Late

I dreamed of Taiaroa
and the sea cliffs outside Dunedin.
I dreamed of albatross.
And how we whispered
when we watched them, nesting.

I woke off balance, could still see
cotton grass dancing in the tussock
and white asphodel.
Snow grass, snow berries
beaded like unwelcome hail.

Then I saw you, clearly,
lying on your side, your bird limbs
drawn to your chin.
The whole of you poised for flight.
Your face, on that smooth pillow,

when I got there
it was already marble.

Josie Walsh

The Funeral at Langho

Hung-over, trying to remember
the once-familiar hymns,
we followed the undertaker's men
as they shouldered your coffin
out into November, out into the wind
which flailed down from the fells,
hurling rooks across the sky,
limp mourning rags,
their high, cracked threnody
drowning out the priest

For months after, I dream of this,
the opening of the vault,
being unable to stop it,
watching you go alone
in the brass-trimmed box
down into that black space,
dream, too, that we're at home
again, you at the kitchen table
in your thick white dressing-gown,
your face turned away.

Polar Bear Daddy back, still angry
with me, and I plead It's not my fault,
it's not my fault.

Angela Kirby

Daughter

Brittle brown leaves disintegrate
on the floor of this bluebell wood,
that slopes down to the marsh –
birch, hazel, sycamore, oak.

From loam layers, the smell of Earth
is a draught of strong ale,
warm huddled cattle,
dark decay becoming matrix
of this fresh young green.

The breeze in the living treetops
seems the breath of her mighty spirit.
Birds flit with it, blithely sing,
in nests their eggs are hatching.

A woodpecker nods its scarlet head,
pecks at a thick trunk,
hops upwards, pecks again, intent.

From this same womb I am,
from soggy, articulate.
My thoughts disintegrate at night,
I wake and look and speak again.

My father's ashes are scattered on Badbury Rings
and I sit on this damp ground
a little stiffly, naming, praising
and getting on.

Dinah Livingstone

Delivery

Tuesday morning, and my mother
is dying again, the tenth
Tuesday since the first and final time

today's bright   replete
with pink mallow day lilies in three
urgent colours, a haze of blue thistle.

The rising sun paints the shadow
of our house's peak on the locusts
where it slowly sets.

In a few hours, I'll feel it all
happen again. I'll be busy
with only a few chores
once ceaseless
left to comfort me

I'm held by peace
I never thought we'd find
like unsuspected honey stored
behind an old house's clapboards

this tenth Tuesday   again
the telephone rings   the words
I knew would come shock me

again a cry   mine?   as I'm
delivered
into another life where no
one remembers   no one knew me

small   hungry   or recalls how
she wanted to feed me but couldn't
this morning she's leaving again
as the red sun soars up   leaving me
a labour as hard as hers

bringing me here

Mary Dingee Fillmore

Grown Up At Last

I dreamed my mother lay smiling in her grave
not the terrible smile of the dead
but her living smile.
The grave was open,
rain was falling in.

Did she smile because nothing could hurt her
not the rain, not her children
bickering as usual
long after the toybox
had passed to theirs?

A C Clarke

Do Not Disturb

No one ever entered although
it wasn't locked.
We furnished it with supposition:
a wardrobe of slippery frocks,
a musky hip-length fur;

a chest of drawers rattled
with bottles of dangerous scent;
a cabinet of papers
that proved origins, ownership;
garments with unexpected holes;

the mattress was stuffed with secrets –
three unsuccessful marriages,
a baffling absence of several months,
some babies lost
through accident or design.

But when we let the light in all we find
is twenty years of birthday cards,
talc and tablecloths still
in see-through packs,
and eleven wooden hangers
with moth-repellent rings attached.

Gill Learner

Legacies

And for you, my rosewood sewing-box,
she said – now it stands, polished and delicate

beside my bed, a neat sarcophagus
in this untidy room, so out of place here

that for weeks I hesitate to open it,
disturb what she last put away

but today I pluck up courage, blowing
off the dust as one who brushes softly

through layers of sand to find small artefacts
in the detritus of a tomb.

What power the everyday possessions
of the dead have to move us –

I finger an ivory spool, a needle-case,
her scissors, silver thimbles,

these twists of silk and cotton thread,
hear her singing Gershwin,

catch the soft, sad, violet scent
of Pivet's Floramie.

Angela Kirby

Quest

Having set out with a scrip and a prayer
beaten a way through overgrown briars
struggled up scarps
misread the map,
I come across it
almost by accident
one wet December night
far from my starting point,
just as I'd dreamed:
the low white wall
the gravel path
the great house with its lighted windows
door shut fast.

I fling my handful of pebbles
against the triple-strengthened glass
watch them trickle back,
press my nose orphan-fashion to the pane
to glimpse the grown-ups having fun
catch an acknowledging eye.

Nothing but static and ice-moon glitter
in a room whose walls go back forever,
no grown-ups after all.

I take a scatter of stones
heap them into a cairn
there on the path

just to declare
to anyone who follows
I made it this far
this far, at least...

A C Clarke

Dumpling

The dumpling's bubbling in the pan
Spicing the air with cinnamon.
I watched Mum mix it, chanting
The ingredients like a charm.
Sugar, ginger, raisins, flour.
Stir it round and make a wish
Toss the lucky silver in
And wield the wooden wand
Hubble bubble with no trouble
A dumpling rich and round.

Now it's I who am Hecate
Keeper of the book of spells.
Read again familiar writing
Feel the catching at my heart
Murmuring the incantation,
Sugar, ginger, raisins, flour
Whisk me to that childhood kitchen.
Conjure up the smells and sounds.
Who'd have thought there'd be such magic
In a dumpling rich and round?

Margaret Wood

First Born
for my mother

My other dead are setting out to greet me,
their sprawling years
weighing them down like clay

but your compacted life, each heartbeat
counted, speeds towards me
light as a bird.

When my time comes, I'll skim across the waves,
follow the scent of that girl pacing the deck,
Suez, Gulf of Arabia, Indian Ocean.

I'll be that self once more under the peepul tree
as I lick the tip of thread for the needle's eye,
stitch the final daisy on your gown.

I won't know, yet, the cataclysm of
that love, the danger of giving
too much too soon.

My hands will cup my tautened belly, catch
the undulations of your limbs
against my palms.

I'll mould my lips into the secret smile,
recover that sense of wonder – the key
to heaven. They'll let me in.

Christine Coleman

Remembering a Future

This house I live in now didn't exist
when you died. Nevertheless I picture
you here in this room: you, Mother, elegant
as always, sit on the sofa and cross
your fine stockinged legs; while you, Dad, standing
there in front of the fire, are saying
(and not for the first time either) 'My word,
it's grand having a room this size!'

For in my memory you've been here often,
and loved the place as I'm still learning to.
And I believe you'll have visited me
wherever I live, your both being dead
no barrier to your inspecting my new
carpets and curtains, or toasting some cheese
in my new kitchen, or testing a bed
in an upstairs not yet built.

I'm glad you come. I'll need you forever:
to admire the views from all my windows,
and to taste for sour or sweet, the apples
from the trees of all my gardens.

Janet Loverseed

Grandmothers

Who Are You?

I wonder what he sees,
am almost unnerved.
Aged five months
he scrutinises me
with puzzled inquiry.
Bold hazel eyes
brighter than blackbird's
slowly take me in.

'It's Granny!' I pipe.
'It's your Granny!'

Suddenly sun bursts
out past cloud,
he smiles
and I know I am.

Dinah Livingstone

Skin

Light shines through
the package in ultra-thin covering
snuggling on my knee.

Firm, plump, soft, embracing
the perfume of a fig that's ripe for eating:
I bury my nose to inhale your sweetness.

Leaning against my breast
and dreaming down the years,
your small, strong fingers fondle mine,

discovering and pulling at
the folds of loose flesh on my hands
that surprise me, unite me

with generations of incredulous women
who learned from the wisdom of their grandchildren
that they were on their way to growing old.

Alwyn Marriage

Scavenging

They lie where they fell:
green armour split cleanly
as with a sword stroke
hurled from the comfort
of silk velvet covers
they gleam in the grass

Two grandmothers
scrabble for treasure
pocket the trove
while each reminds each
that it's just for the little'uns
for Katie for Peter
for Joe Luke and Leah
for Jervais
for Jake

All children
love conkers

Joy Howard

Bellchildren

Lavinia spoke. 'They warm your heart,
these children from your flesh and blood.'
That rang a bell. My mother said,
'I'll never rear her.' But she did.
She lost her mother early on,
went searching for her ever since.
A ruined life's a sad affair.
My flawed old heart is knocking on.
It needs the glow of filial care.
Just like a clock it marks the hours
while counting down and wearing out,
as church bells ring to ward off storms,
extinguish fires, spin devils off.
I hear the chimes which drive the beat
as echoes of what's gone before.
While on the grass these children play,
they laugh and call and sing in time.
Such small inspectors claiming love.
Facsimiles in miniature,
the clear-eyed gaze of long ago.
I'm past. They're present, future years.
The story must go on and on.
As weeks roll by, it helps to know
these infants' ways take cadence from
this rocking cradle of my heart.

Jenny Morris

The Ruby Bird
for my stepmother

Owl babies whimper deep inside the privet,
says my little granddaughter,
and I want to believe her outrageous ornithology.

Her big sister suggests it's the sound of the wind
or a lone seagull lost in Morningside,
but here without curtains to shut out the night,

I know better. This sound is tousle-feathered
like visiting grandmothers –
like you Ruby bird, hunched in your tatters

that ruffled so easily as you slipped into senility.
As your famous bullshit detectors turned
to paranoia, we were all guilty of something.

We could not protect you from the naked glass,
that reflected only pain.
Not owl babies, I whisper

when they are washed, kissed, sleep-breathing,
what you hear is the Ruby bird.
Undeterred by the jaundiced glare

of the sodium vapour street lamp,
she shields visiting grandmothers –
spreads her wings, grey with time.

Wendy Klein

31

Becoming
for Eva

Daddy calls you Princess and you're longing
for the whole pink-satin-bodices-with-bows,
stardust Disney thing,
with of course the handsome prince,
who'll have more hair than Daddy,
and a horse.

But think...
do you want to end up slung across a saddle
never handling the reins yourself,
or clean and cook for seven little men
then be poisoned with an apple?
Could you bear to be abducted
by a dragon?

Would you wish to wed a man
more simple than his cat;
to be a pawn in bargainings with Beasts
or diminutive-but-cunning tailors?
Could you let a wily servant trick you into
minding geese?

Imagine hospitality
involving twenty mattresses piled above a pea,
or dancing secretly
while a smart-arse soldier spies on you.
And let's not even think
about the frog.

So…
aim to skipper England's football squad,
conduct the last night of the Proms, direct the BBC.
And dare we hope
one day to see a woman
Primate of all England
or even Pope?

Gill Learner

Under the Influence
for Jay

Grandparenthood addles the brain.
How else to explain
that I intone
'Nee-nah, nee-nah'
at the sight of a police car
even when I'm out walking alone.

Gill Learner

Jack Discovers Impermanence

'If you cut off my head,' he asks, aged four,
'what would you see?'

So we talk.
About blood and bones, and tubes
for the food and air to go down.

'And if you burnt me all up,' he asks,
'what would happen?'

So we talk.
About ash rising fine
on the wind, a butterfly's wing
to flirt with the sun.

'And where would I be?' he asks.

So we talk.
About the completely untenable
no-Jack hypothesis.
A world without Jack to see it,
a not-even-space where Jack has been.

'But Jesus came back,' he says,
'when he'd died. He rose
from the dead. They told us at school.'

So we talk.
About beautiful stories,
and what grandmas don't know.

And I want to say:
'In this life, boy, you hang on tight,
push off, and swing into space,
not knowing where you will land. Or whether.'

And I want to say:
'Reach for the light,
but don't think you can hide there.
It's for seeing, not escaping.'

And I want to say:
'Sit with the mystery, unknowing.
The only thing certain is now,
and that's pretty improbable.'

And I want to say:
'I love you, small speck
of thistledown, spinning off
into the dark.'

Instead I ask:
'And did you read today
to Mrs Ferguson?'

Pat Simmons

Grand-play

Which dolly will you have?
                              she asks.
her eyes so sharp
they pierce my heart,
and sentenced to this time together,
I'm forced to choose.

The one with curly hair,
                              I say,
she frowns,
picking up the other one,
the frowsy blonde,
with an air of disdain.

Shall we swap?
                              she asks.
and I'm forced to agree,
afraid not to,
seeing the ghost of her mother's disapproval
in the curve of her lips,
in her pointed chin:
in her narrowed eyes:
something steely.

Wendy Klein

36

Taking Over the Night Shift

Too nervous to relax and lying stiffly
on my side in my daughter's bed, I face
my tiny grandson asleep in his cot.
Will he not miss her touch, her smell, her face,
her gentle voice?

He wakes at one and four, eating his hands
between each crying fit. I make haste
down to the kitchen for his milk, but,
when I reappear, he's waiting patiently
as though he knows I'll bring him what he needs.

In my arms he sucks efficiently
although from time to time he lets the teat
slip from his mouth so he can smile at me
and make baby noises which I take to mean
'I say, old girl, don't you find all this
most awfully jolly?' Enchanted,
I smile back at him and say
'Oh I do, my love, I do, I do. But let's
have less of the "old girl" nonsense!'
He makes a low-down giggle in his throat,
which makes me laugh. Our merry conversations
take so long that each feed lasts an hour.

Around midday tomorrow, his mother
will return. I can sleep for hours. Will she want me
for a night shift again? Have we been too
shockingly sociable, her son and I?
Shall I tell her?

Janet Loverseed

Dunadh

These are the treasures of one small child:

How he makes play with my polished stones
Placing each one with infinite delicacy
In the dinky toy pick-up
That was his father's

How he takes himself off into the quiet
Opens a book and unfolds a story
Like a little bard
Solemn, transported

How he studies my face when I ask him
If he could please give me back my glasses
And he says quite sweetly
'I couldn't.'

How I feel his skinny little ribs
When I squeeze him and tickle him
And kiss his soft hair
Which glitters red-gold

How he laughs like a tiny old man
Who has seen and heard almost everything
And is surprised to find
Anything still funny

How when I hold him I hold his
Tow-headed two-year-old father

Who holds himself stiffly now
In my embrace

These are treasures of one small child

Elisabeth Rowe

Weekends with Leah

These visits are a string of beads
all sizes and all colours: glitter and gleam
threaded on silver, sometimes gold.

Though careful search may find
traces of blood from a needle-prick
or tough knots made to keep
a breaking sequence whole,

through blue of birth to diamond white
rose damask and pearl grey, in shimmer
or in stillness they give back the light
that made them; making age-weary eyes
a mirror for love, for the dearness of life.

Joy Howard

39

Macedoine

A thin film of syrup running down the
plump slope of a ripe pear, too good
to wipe clean. Two orange pippins

bursting into a champagne pop.
She is laughing. Lifting her from
her crib I bury my nose in her velvet

roundness, her scent of raspberry
and boysenberry, teasing her into
more pops, more bubbles, more fizz

as she struggles to break free. I am damp
from her, my face blotched with her juices,
my hair sticky in her honeysuckle clasping.

She is all the warmth of harvest, all the
lightness of Spring. 'I am your Grannie'
I whisper against her tumbleweed head.

'I am your candles and your songline. I am
your storyteller and your painter. I am
your secret root, your crumbled ground.'

Hilary Elfick

Embodiment

How beautiful each tree
full-bodied in July,
growing and itself
each year against the sky.

The purple copper beech –
no wine so rich and dark –
stands on the green hill
above the boating lake.

The body thickening
with sixty-seven years,
as does its consciousness
of what it sees and hears.

Connecting more to more,
memory and rhythm
body-history senses
aware their night must come.

My birthday and my grandson's
both fall in July –
what I love seen fresh
by his bright learning eye.

Dinah Livingstone

Looking After

They arrive in a tsunami rush, drop debris
in their wake. The flood rises to the rooms
under the roof, floats out stored
                                        dolls,
                        crayons,
            cars,
                                from floor to floor.
Mornings begin with gull-calls overhead,
scrabbling on the stairs. Days
pass at different levels,
measured in gaps from meal to meal.

Danger waits in every room:
a nail-file, an unsteady stool.
It's not activity that drains
but vigilance.
            At last
there's supper, baths, bed-time
spun out with stories   kisses
promises for morning.
Then short hours to slump
before skin-deep sleep,
one ear on 'monitor'.
            After goodbyes,
the ebb sucks vigour from the house.
I drift   find   odd socks here
a comic there.
Restless as the moon
I listen for the call that says
they're home.
            Now,
I occupy the quiet, tidy hours,
and wait
for the hole of their not-being-here
to fill.

Gill Learner

The great big bed in Grandma's hotel room

Ryo bounces   Ryo bounces
Ryo forward-rolls

Lui bounces   Lui bounces
tries to forward-roll

Grandma watches   Grandma winces
Grandma foretells falls

Ryo scampers   Lui scampers
out into the night

Grandma falls in bed exhausted
mumbling night night   night ni...

Gina Shaw

Peter's Bus

Peter drives a lower case bus
we cannot go upstairs
he has a little ticket machine
for when we pay our fares

soon he'll grow up and when he does
his bus will be big and wide
we'll go upstairs and see for miles
and we'll all have a Capital ride

Gina Shaw

A Poem Called Katie

write a poem called Katie
she said
so

I'll put in those tights
which gallop her legs down the Close
and land her on my doorstep
where she clatters at my letter-box

two very blue bright eyes peering through
to check whether I'm coming
and the jiggles and giggles
when she sees me

the shoes and coat she throws off
in the hall
before she takes command of my living-room

(there won't be a cardigan
she'll have left it at school   again)

a landslide of paper pencils paints glue scissors stickers
which send her into an ecstasy of humming

many imaginary babies which she unzips
from her tummy and which I
have to pretend to feed
before she zips them back in again
along with blankets cots bottles bears

my daughter's stubbornness
not yet fully flowered

my temper ditto

and a special ingredient
which can't be identified
but for the time-being
must be known as
a poem called Katie

Gina Shaw

Grandchildren

may they be born
and they will be perfect

may they know what they want
and get it

may they grow up

may they want what they get
and it be right and good

may they live

may they outlive

Gina Shaw

In a Flash

You hand me a photograph, and in it,
your chin, with its five-o'clock shadow
is a foil to the tender cheek
of your first-born

But wait, it is only a moment since
you were the baby, lying on my bed,
staring curiously sideways,
as if getting to know the wallpaper,
or working out some plan.

You'll notice how quickly it all happens.
The photos fly in and out of the albums
like snow, like melting snow.

Connie Bensley

46

Mind the Gap

Down the Line

Is this what it's about after forty years –
letting them
      hold the fort
           bear the brunt
                watch and wait
while we take up new lives?

They keep our grandchildren
      in trust
           on loan
and through them earn
      a whisper of far-off music
           glimpses down the shining line
              a hint of things to come.

Now it's their turn
      to fidget in the dark
           straining ears
              as the clock spits out the pips of hours
while the future
      finds its feet
           learns the steps
              and whistles different tunes.

Gill Learner

Not On Display

She views us through fashion shades,
two penguins plumped on the pool side,
mangy zoo birds cloaked in striped towels
instructed to tuck in frayed or floppy bits,
cover bodies that, displayed,
will floor her just as once
her sticky tantrums flattened us.

Is it his puffed belly and silver face fuzz
or my brown-spotted, high-veined hands,
puckered thighs, post-Caesarean overhang
that crease her so? Eleven years old,
mounting the narrow catwalk of puberty,
she'd like to cut the flab, model us in styles
worthy to view through fashion shades.

June Hall

Thirty Years On

Now that I'm blind,
I see things more clearly
my father used to say.

Thirty years on
I can see the sense of that.
Things could be worse,
there are compensations,
for instance, everyone
making allowances
because of my age
and failing sight

but it's hard on the children.
I hear it in their voices –
already those notes
of weary patience
though usually
they make a joke of it.
All right there, Mother?
Enjoying your dinner?

They're scared, of course,
already wondering
just which of them
will be stuck with me
at the end.

Angela Kirby

Journey

Someone is dying on the mountain
as the train passes.
All week snow has been creeping lower
down the glens;
Spring is frozen in a foxy haze of
buds in waiting;
I am leaving, perhaps this is why
it hurts so much
when this slip of a girl sitting opposite
gives me the look.
I ask her quite politely to move from
my reserved seat
and she does, with a venomous glare
of mingled scorn
and indifference. Outside the window
the great hills unwind
southwards, a string of lochs and peaks
blurred by our breath
on the cold window, and my eyes watering
with something like shame.

I study the girl's face for a softening
but her chin is set
at an angle of sassy assertiveness, her eyes
are glacier mints.
And then suddenly she flashes a beatific smile
at the small child
sitting next to me, and I know it is personal.
She wants me to see
myself as old and irrelevant. I should be
above all this, but
what is the wisdom of years beside the raw
certainty of youth?

I am near the end of my journey: *timor mortis*
conturbat me.
I will the girl to get out at the next station
and she does, leaving
her friend curled up back to the misted window
and the mountains
and the man unknown to us dying up there
alone in the snow.

Elisabeth Rowe

The Oasis

Meadowhall on Monday morning.
      Elderly couples and pairs of friends
in pastel blouses and elasticated skirts
      circulate in a hesitant waltz
to *Around the World in Eighty Days,*
      the canned music mocking
their progress across the frontage
      of Zizzi, KFC, Pizza Express.
I leave my coffee and stand at the railing
      to watch that bright, courageous
promenade around the tables.

Carole Bromley

Street-wise

They lilt through fag packets and fast-food trash
on polished pins, knee-backs mapped, ankles
resolute. In wanton skirts they take living
in their stride: boots gappy around calves
or zipped like second skins. Cling-film denim,
artfully rubbed pale, skims tightly convex bellies
between bony crests. Hands with flowered
or spangled nails fasten chat to ears while
pique or empathy are fluent, loud.

Did we once seem as confident, as careless
of the easy slip of time? Our friendships hung
on coppers for call-boxes; pen, paper, stamps.
Nights in were Goons or Glums or *What's my line?*;
out, youth club socials or the flicks.

Now I catch my smile in a shop window:
I don't covet their allure or begrudge
the busy clamour of their youth but
I must admit I envy them their teeth.

Gill Learner

Generation Gap

Arm yourself with all the steel you like,
you'll never be safe in this place.
This is foreign. Not the nice front
kept smart for casual callers. This
is the bit behind the main square,
those dark alleys that lead
to gut-wrenching squalor.
You don't belong here, yet here you are,
trying to speak the language.
You find the words change overnight,
even the meaning of the words,
so what you say is not what you meant to say.
How to behave? Whoever makes the rules
it isn't you. Listen to
the sniggering at each silly slip.
Guide books won't help. They only tell
how you might have got through yesterday,
when it was all different. Even
the maps have changed. You're lost.
You panic, make things worse.
Sensing your panic, they
close in. You are disarmed.

Ann Alexander

For my Son on his Birthday

I

Nearly three decades ago – no slapping needed
for those first lungfuls –
you met the world head on.

They gave you to me, wrapped and peaceful,
a smear of blood over your left eyebrow.

Only your fingers moved
clutching fistfuls of air.

II

Your arms are muscled now, have lost the creases
of newness. You embrace me like a stranger
uncertain of the right way to behave.

I guess in your eyes my own resentments
recycled. When I speak to you I hear
my mother's voice.

III

Watching your fingers light a cigarette,
I want to rearrange your history,
where nothing keeps its former place.

It is hard to remember how things were
debris of both our futures strewn across
what once was familiar.

IV

Unmet needs chasm between us.
We cannot hear ourselves
across the gap.

But we are tied
by filaments which cling
spiderfast.

A C Clarke

Elegy for Lives Gone by Too Fast

We never got around to albums.
We put the children in a tin,
put that on a shelf,
and now someone has binned the children
and the light bulbs are downed with dust
though we are still alive
and somewhere in the house.

We always wanted to give them more.
It's gone too far, too fast.
Forgive the dust.

Diane Tang

The Grey-haired Woman Dead-heads Her Roses

I am afraid in the streets,
they are too full, crowded with feral girls.
Sinuous, otter-sleek, they brush past me,
the breath slipping, sweet as alyssum,
between their small, cruel teeth.

I see them dance and sway
down pavements, gutters, watch
their sapling spines spin to a morning wind,
hear them sing their harsh new words
to my old music.

I am wounded, cut deep
by the sharpness of their eyes.
Such girls, I imagine them turned soft,
turned smooth, twisting supple as green vines
round the hard thighs of their lovers.

Safe here in my garden,
drained of colour by the recent drought,
I watch them pass,
rake the dust a little
and tear the heads from dying roses.

Angela Kirby

To a Young Woman

Listen. I am old, sister child.
I remember Suez, my first glimpse of mortality.
The man on the corner would call out death
before we all had television and could turn off.
I saw my own face in the mirror of his breath.

Before you shouted your first protest
stretched your first lung   before you
taught yourself to withdraw
I was wandering in a wilderness too cold for locust
or honey. I too was looking for translation,
looking to learn the local tongue.

When you were inside her arms
sucking at your first mother's breast
I had bought a ticket North, my own iron
and fled the pelican nest. There I learnt to kiss
upside down, to wear lampshades on my head.
There I slept on floorboards in a forest, I
climbed a hill of cars and learnt by letter
about death.

While you counted building bricks and clattered
in short socks feeding ducks and pigeons in the park
I have wept before redheaded children who smiled
and broke me. I have danced for praise and money
into the empty eyeful dark.

Listen. I am old, sister child.
my grey hair was earnt.
My torn eyes have seen me crack mirrors
my tired mouth sucked these fingers when they burnt.
I remember long empty years when I reproduced
myself time after time after time. I circled dizzy
with the dust that fluffed my fears.

I remember my shrinking heart, now obstinate,
and falter. Where did I learn to beat it strong?
My hand was always full of warning; though
someone whispered once the line of life was long
I knew the pictures and the numbers never matched.
It was a thing I couldn't alter.

Only in aeroplanes when I looked down on clouds
and glaciers could I forget how much I'd cried.
Only with wrists in running water cold as ice
could I forget the frozen years I sometimes died.

I am old, sister child.
Each day was hacked in me
scratched in me with a penknife dipped in brine.
I cried on my birthday
I doubted my mother
I avoided my father's eyes
I betrayed friends
I stole, got lost, told my lover lies
I died many little deaths
when you were being born.

All this takes time.

Berta Freistadt

Gap Year

My god-daughter, an idealistic child
who, it appears, learnt nothing from me,
is doing good works in North London,
Enfield to be precise, also taking in Barnet
and the wilder reaches of Camden.
In return for my reluctant sponsorship
she sends breathless round robins
with multiple exclamation marks
and an optimism about human nature
that makes my eyes water. In between
taking the Lord to gangs of hoodies
and running a praise group for a woman
who's too pregnant to stand
she does a soup run for the homeless
and has already had offers of marriage!!!!
Her mentor, a lad of twenty-one,
has a burning need to tell the story
of his death and rebirth in Jesus.
He sends me a card. I can't think
who I know that has that handwriting,
unless it's an ex-pupil from 10XG.
He loves the whole world, this boy
and is especially fond of himself.
He tells me, in overexcited prose!!!
that he'll never forget that day
just as there are still *some very old people*
who can tell you where they were
the day President Kennedy was killed.

Carole Bromley

61

Old Lady Rap

Hey boy, just cos my teeth ain't my own,
you think I got nothin to say. Well,
you're wrong, boy, you are all the way wrong.

Just cos my arthritis makes me bent and stiff,
you think I'm slow, I'm feeble. Well,
you're wrong, boy. I am in pain, all the day pain,
and that makes me one mean mutha.

Don't you write me off yet, treating me like a Spaz,
I may be a withered old skank, but I ain't finished yet.

Just cos I'm deaf, don't shout, young man,
take your dummy-tit out your mouth and
ar-ti-cu-late.

Don't think you can teach an old bitch new tricks.
I've seen it all before, boy, ain't nothin new about you.

Hey boy? You think you're finished?
You think you can mess with me?
You think you ain't got nothin to lose?

You think you can show me pain?
You just a puppy dog!
I'll give you somethin to worry about,
somethin to remember me by.

I'm gonna mess with your head,
I'm gonna laugh you out of my house,
I'm gonna show you the mean little squit you are.
Bring it on, boy, I ain't scared of you.

I lookin death in the face every day,
and He the Man,
He the mean muthafucka.

He comin for you too, pretty boy.

Rosemary McLeish

Beauty Counter

The Eldorado of the Eastgate Centre beckons.
I head for Debenham's, a trinket box of
glittering treasures. I step inside,
walk through summer meadows
crushing petals beneath my feet.
Behind banks of bottled potions
sloe-eyed temptresses
wave scarlet tips in my direction.
I am iron filings to their magnet.

Transform my skin to dew-kissed roses,
drown my eyes in pools of aquamarine
fringed about with midnight.
Take this base metal and practise your art
of alchemy. Wave your magic wands of
Kissable Pink, Sherbet Dab or *Hot
Sex on a Saturday Night* and turn it into gold.
Or, failing that, I'll have a jar of cold cream.

Margaret Wood

Sick and Tired

Untimely

A rope tightens rough around my chest
as I breathe in my bare-topped children,
brush their summer skin, smell their smallness.

Willow arms trail sleep across the bed,
fingers floating towards his teddy. Beside him
his twiggy sister sprawls, drooped on an edge.

These long-limbed saplings need me
firm-rooted and, as in this vigil, still – not
quivering, shaken with disease, old too soon.

The time is out of synch like a match
that burns too fast, searing fingers
when the flame goes out, candles not yet lit.

June Hall

Waiting Room

In the doctor's waiting room
we discuss the weather –
half-way through December
but still as mild as May –
pooling unseasonable roses,
bulbs, geraniums
while just imagine,
one of us is suffering
from a rush of clematis to the hedge
so I throw in my plumbago
and boast about its agonising blue.

Despite this,
Christmas threatens,
the magazines are full of it.
All is glitter, candles, tinsel, glass,
amongst the dubious promises
of evergreens
and the windows have broken out
in a rash of cotton wool.

Recalled for further tests
I turn the pages,
half-listening to something
that my body wants to tell me
but I may not wish to hear –
the signals seem familiar
yet there's a different twist –
odd that pregnancy and this
should share so many symptoms –
sickness, swelling,
small unspecific pains.

Not up to feeling festive
and wary of wreaths
I discard Christmas
to pick another magazine,
Interiors
which sounds more likely
to concentrate the mind.

Angela Kirby

Thwart 1

It gathers in me
a thunderstorm brewing
in my bones my skin my cells

Heavier I slow down
cumuli and sleet
running through me
hailstones drumming in my veins
filling up the passages
once inhabited by tussocks of light

Hard hard legs
chest arms head
all choked
with heavy weather

Berta Freistadt

The Shake

Not even
   a spilt cup of tea.
      Everyone's hand shakes
   sometimes,
doesn't it?
   Mine used to –
     before.
   Is it better?
you ask,
   Is it worse?
      sneaking a look.
Not much
   on view.

      Getting good at deception.

Right hand
   protects the other,
 holds, enfolds,
     substitutes, hides
      – above all
    hides –
like a mother
 who covers for a
   wayward child
 yearns to restore
the peace
   yet fails.

Left hand
  restrained
    at night
  in the intruder's grip
    shudders,
  wild to regain

      the norm of day.

Legacy

Through her camouflage of mohair
my fingers meet a sudden shoulder blade
and jut of rib. Bone of her bone is nothing new.
Flesh of her flesh. But this is new:
that stem cells of a foetus make their way
into the very marrow of their host –
renew themselves, year after year. So
I transmit my thoughts, electric pulses along
axons and dendrites out through my palms
and fingertips into her skin then down
to the dark centre of bone where my own
cells and my siblings' cells and the cells of our
long-dead brother, her first baby, jostle each other
and I tell them *push your strength into her.*

Christine Coleman

Medical Examination

Red cells : eleven plus.
Skin : two-hundred lines.
Thyroid needs a resit.

Breathing: could do better.
Artwork : rushed homework.
Liver : inattention;
oil could do with changing.

Practicals : sluggish.
Back a blotch of smudges;
are we talking Finals?

Grit in cranial crankshaft.

Medical student sits me on chair;
observes with clinical interest
how my feet don't reach the ground.

Driving home
I stroke my calves between the changes.
        There there, don't take no notice;
        lovely you are, my lovelies,
        and he's a nasty man.
Insuring my strengths.

Over cocoa consider my results.
Conclude too soon to start revising.

Hilary Elfick

No Easy Way

There is no easy way of silencing
your screaming skin. In unaccustomed folds
it cloaks protruding bones, tissue-thin
and sagged with loss of muscle tone.

An echo of that crooked, sexy smile
drifts past your face, storm cloud or sail
bellied before the wild October wind
which leaves, on passing, traces in the sand

outside your window. Seated there, behind
the insulating glass, you contemplate
the elements. I long to hold you, wait
and, motionless, unwittingly recall

the gentle warmth of your sure fingers. They
are turning into driftwood as I look,
or coral, spiky, bleached, ready to break
in needle splinters at a glance. The sea

has not yet chilled your eyes, although it laps
along the foreshore, creeping closer till
it meets them, then receding; but your lips
still shine, sleek pearl of empty mussel shells.

In gull-sharp shrieks your skin protests the touch
of whistling winds or lover's fingertips
alighting feather-soft upon your hands
but calms at the swift shadow of a kiss.

Lyn Moir

Entering Alzheimers

From the far shore where the herring gulls bred
he turned without understanding their cries
to search for something that he remembered.

Like the twining of fingers as she led
him to watch the rain skeining the skies
from the far shore where the herring gulls bred.

The dread in her eyes as their bodies, sated,
cooled in the night air. Now her face, misplaced, defies
his search. Something that he remembered?

Thoughts that would not untangle, that fled
with the flash of fish silver-slipping by
from the far shore where the herring gulls bred.

When he tried to snare words, in their stead
came sounds without form, sounds that disguised
his search for something that he remembered.

Now, unclear, fearing that even when he is dead
memory, shape shifting, will not distinguish lies
from the far shore where the herring gulls bred
to search for something that he remembered.

Ruth O'Callaghan

And none says what is right or beautiful

Dementia rifles the phone book.
We think it is about fading away,
but it is the earth draws closer,
come to embrace the living,
disencumber them of bills and passbooks.

Travelling light, the familiar one
leaves in the uncalled taxi
and the mocking one appears,
says I don't know *you*.
With clinical care, with slow anger
we care for the mummy
dumped on the doorstep.

Desire squeezed out like a lemon,
as we knew it should but could not.
A hand is a hand is a hand:
maybe earth is the name of a dance.
Leastways, the moon
never cared to know my ID.

Pleasance, art teacher, peace activist,
silent, cared for, recognising nothing
but her wildflowers picked in a Devon field.
I think what ruts I run in. What flowers I know.

Pamela Coren

Whatever it was he said…

something about how I'd been
so graceful, so physical
how I'd loved to dance.

Sitting on the sofa not mean
hearted, just interested, concerned.
Question after question, no answer
to most. I don't know, Brian,

I don't know. Then you know
how it is when you're thinking
about the end of the world…
wet all over Sue's jumper.

Whatever it was he said.

Berta Freistadt

We Two

Prankish like Puck, invisible,
it flutters the print I'm reading,
jitters me with nerve-piercing noise,
shivers my flesh with ice chills.

It intrudes in love-making like
the South Wind at play in the sun
and, when I'm driving, takes the wheel
in sterner mood, arm heavy on mine.

Down the long blind alley of night
it lurks to ambush sleep,
jumps me, half-Nelsons my arm,
squeezes and clamps my leg taut.

Sometimes though it tires, pleads
for me to soften, smile within its grip,
stroke the arm it teases,
hold the hand it's colonised until

I can imagine folding to my care
my self.

June Hall

Arrhythmia

Yesterday, a frightened blackbird flew
into our kitchen through the open door

and could not find, at first, the way to leave.
Helpless, I watched it struggle for an hour,

saw how it hurled itself against the panes
with flailing wings, blinded by its despair.

Now as I lie awake throughout the night,
here in the curving hollow of your arm

and catch the reckless rhythms of your heart,
I am reminded of the bird's alarm,

of how its flutterings would fail and start
again, before it made it to the calm

cool glide-paths of the outside air once more.
You sleep, and do not know that I (as if

such gentling could keep you safe from harm)
silently kiss your lips, your eyes, your hair.

Angela Kirby

Inside the Mirror

Inside the mirror you're settled for the night,
your head tucked into the dip of the pillow,
your hands drawn up, just touching your face.
The light that's kept on for you all night, now,
falls on the curve of your shoulder, smoothing
its green cotton. I take off my shoes, lean
towards the mirror, achieve the exact angle
to hide your cannula, your oxygen tank,
the tackle of your survival. My fingers,
which are practised in touching your skin,
your sleeves – tender even towards your buttons –
undress me quickly: I don't need to break
my gaze from that framed world where your breath
comes and goes, easy, as strong as mine.

Christine Webb

Like a Formal Feeling
for Jan (after Emily Dickinson)

This summer of eating for two
was like no other – not like the first time,
so full of nausea and terror, watching
my marks fall; my weight rise –
or the second, not believing my luck
at the way it happened so soon, so easily,
dreaming a son, delighting in a daughter –
or even the very last time – nearly too late,
my hands on my belly, pleading, *live, live, live.*

This summer was different because it was you,
my old friend, un-safely outside my body,
the two of us connected by a tangled network
of shared history – you, attached to a thousand
tubes, nil by mouth day after day, week after
baffling week; your beautiful bones startled
into visibility as flesh fell away from your face,
arms, thighs and calves, their restless fretting
on the air bed intended to prevent bedsores,

and me wringing my hands, helpless until I found
my vocation in listening to your dreams of food,
transforming them into fantasy feasts at your bedside,
feeding them to you course by tantalising course –
pink grapefruit afternoons, swapped later for
mango juice, Egyptian-style – your brief obsession
with lasagne; with or without the Sicilian fillip
of anise, whether to find a shop that sold
Italian ricotta or settle for Sainsbury's curd.

If I dressed in white like blessèd Emily,
sipped lemon tea, composed my lines
in a delicate spidery hand, would I be saying how
we *noticed smallest things – things*
overlooked before…italicised as – 'twere?
Would I be scribbling painstaking verses
on whether death might stop – kindly
or not – sooner than either of us expected?
After great pain, a formal feeling comes.

Wendy Klein

Dark Matter

Some days, I can't summon up a smile.
Blaming you for the journey you've been forced
to make, I automate my answers, nod,
sweep through rooms on a mission, ticking lists.
Tenderness, caresses, our long interrogative
gaze – vanished down some mineshaft
of the past. What evidence emerges
is peripheral – sheets hung, bread cut,
soup ladled, and the house not so much
run as levered from waking to sleeping.
This is dark matter, only to be inferred
by its effects on what surrounds it: if
it's love, there'll be a day to be thankful.

Christine Webb

Good Loving

April

How lily-of-the-valley
with its spear leaves, flowers
even through tarmac.

How he, dressed in his old greens,
cuts new grass, makes
shine and shadow lines
across its breadth and length.

How this month marks
fifty years and still
she scarcely knows him.

How when April comes,
it still surprises.

Josie Walsh

Larder

In case this harvest doesn't last, I'll set something by:
fire a drum of applewood to smoke split kisses;
fillet laughter, pack it into pots with oil and herbs.
I'll seal your voice in shiny tins, string private jokes
and dry them, press a bunch of your best anecdotes.

Your hangovers will feed the compost heap, along
with crossness when I come home late, flu-induced
self-pity, a taste for horror films. And I'll throw on
football absences and Leonard Cohen times.

But against the day the cornucopia runs out,
I'll have a hoard: memories of Norway layered in salt;
whispers distilled in tiny bottles; vacuum-packs
of secret looks; nights simmered in honeydew, poured
into jars and stored where the sun shines through.

Gill Learner

The Circle

The site's not marked upon our map
while the suggested route, up and across
a wind-whipped hill, is difficult to see
and even worse to climb. Six wrong turns,
three dead ends, our clothing snagged
and torn by wire and brambles,
you're growing blasphemous, but yet
although the day's a sod I won't give up.
The last farm falls away, we push through scrub,
a group of sullen cattle, and suddenly it's there,
the circle, seven stones haunched against the sky.
You linger by a gate, point out the dangers,
how we could sprain an ankle,
break a leg, and not be found for hours
or even days. You're right, of course
but, sweetheart, think, not so far ahead
you and I will share the safety of the grave
so while we can, let's take these crazy leaps
from clump to sinking clump of grass
and trust me, love, this one time more.
Being country born, well-used to quagmires,
now all these decades on, though stiff
and not so sure of foot, I still can find a way
to cross the bog and reach this place
that's taken both of us so long to find.

Angela Kirby

Morning

Waking at first light
I notice with surprise
that you have grown old:
beneath your bluish pale
transparent skin
I see the skull
tightening its grip;
your breath
comes so thinly
I think you are dead.

I press the lobe of your ear
until you stir
then leave you
in the cluttered dreams
that come at dawn;
outside the window
roses have turned to paper
overnight; a bird
scatters the same notes
again and again.

I listen to the strong pulse
of the earth,
learn the fluidity
of things, how nothing
holds to its proportion:

the song of a thrush
filling the morning
right to its edge;
love shrinking to a small
tight knot of fear.

Elisabeth Rowe

When

the plain light fades
to a memory of light

and you can't find its root
which was always only ever in you,

I don't want the gentle hands of strangers to lift you.
I want it to be me that cups

your head, so your skull nests
and your neck shivers like a tiny sigh of satisfaction.

This is what old is, when every leaf is as new as the last
and the poplars are bronzed as young helmets.

Only open, I say to my empty hand,
only open.

Kate Foley

Nothing

Even if we do nothing,
I want the length of you
pressed to me, cheek to toe
and skin to skin.

And while we do nothing,
lying quietly and breathing
mouth to mouth, I want
your hand along my thigh.

And if nothing turns to
something, well and good
and as it should be, but
if not, I need you still

as part of me.

Lyn Moir

Sleeping Together

'To sleep with' has become a euphemism
For fucking, humping, shagging, or whatever
Leads to orgasm, to the spurt of jism
That signals 'tools down' for the jobbing lover.
Sleeping with someone is an act of love –
Another phrase that raises nudge and wink
When it is innocently spoken of –
Though not erotic as the dullards think.
Sleeping is quiet time for private study;
A heaven-given opportunity
Of cherishing another human body
In all its perilous proximity,
Its promontories and its recesses,
The busy music of its processes.

Ann Drysdale

By Heart

Shaped sounds that leave their pot-pourri perfume
lingering in empty rooms,
melting into beeswax polish, curling
and swirling in mists of incense.

Folk tales, childhood incantations, favourite
scripture passages that have no need
to play on lips or echo in the chambers of the ear;
words repeated until their meaning drains away,

while sinking deeper, tender in the tinder of the heart;
and though their repetition conveys no information
can still surprise as echoes of hidden music
rise up through the mundane and familiar.

Words known more deeply than thought or memory,
creating in secret the context of identity:
important, trivial words that change the world,
like *goodnight*, and *I love you*.

Alwyn Marriage

At Home
for Hugh

The man across the ward has a pot plant
and a television set and now his wife
has brought a little reading lamp. They close
his curtains and sit quiet in their fantasy home.

It must be cosy in there: the trolleys' clanging
muffled, and the bleeps of chemo machines
pushed to a far distance, to another world
where they have chosen not to live.

We do not have such organising energy.
We're scared to gather a fabric tomb around us.

So we sit, me skewed and awkward, neck cricked
by hospital furniture arrangements,
you curled in the whispering womb of the ripple bed,
and we hold each other's hands, our only home

in this new grey land where we did not choose to live.
Between our palms we hold our privacy, the space
where love and warmth can nestle and a thousand
little jokes we do not need to tell.

And when I leave there are no walls to hide
the fierce and gentle glory of our kiss.

Pat Simmons

93

For Finbar, in December

I watch the sunset and imagine you;
I watch the moon come up and think of you.

When rain ghosts from the west,
I think of it as gift;
the butterfly that settles on my naked foot
in August heat brings messages.

And in this month, each year
I come to you,
crossing the water that divides us
till my feet touch land.

I come to you now with flowers,
lay them gently on your quilt of grass.

In the private silence of this cemetery
I tell you everything.

Gill McEvoy

Where's the Steeple?

How do I know your hands
tell me the truth? Because
mine cannot lie.

Stripped of carefulness
in the strong disinfectant of truth
they're naked, no longer ready

for easy, familiar gestures,
for wooing or soothing
when they should fall silent in my lap.

When your hand crept cold,
sweaty, trembling, into mine,
no words were said,

but mine, trembling back,
confirmed the invitation.
Your hands are limber,

nimble, good at making
gothic steeples,
while mine make roman arches,

but used to the last resource
of touch, each neuron fired,
fingers speaking in tongues,

our hands lie, resting quietly
after the work of love,
in the earned interlace of silence.

Kate Foley

Even Then

your hair glowed fewer
colours, only soft gold
and bronze

your breasts were high
and stiff, did not billow
beneath my fingers

the skin near your neck stretched
thick and tight, unlike
today's crepe silk

and your face then
uncharted, where now
every path tracks long love

oh yes I already loved you
even then

Mary Dingee Fillmore

Compensations in a Yellow Light

> *O, sir! you are old:*
> *Nature in you stands on the very verge*
> *Of her confine.*
> Shakespeare: *King Lear*

Collar the girl in the shop
to reach the impossible packet on the shelf
and then to put it back
if it's wrong. And to tell *you*, Thank you.

Full five yards down from the junction
crab your way across the street
one slow step at a time. Stick up!
if horn should bleat or window grimace.

On beautiful startling calendars
in every corner of the house
mark this moment's thought before the next
evaporates it off. Feel it here

when you turn the yellow light on
(though brainball sweats and shrinks inside its shell
and curses room and desk and lamp to hell) –
the small familiar jolts of desire. And here –

the stubborn flutter at the breastbone like hands
pounding out a signal on an upturned hull.
For today, my love, the sea,
the cold bitter sea is suddenly sunstruck.

Diane Tang

Not Exactly a David

You stood in welcome, arms outstretched,
muscled as he was, skin darkened to teak
by years of wind, lacking only patina
from crowds stroking your thighs, feeling
for imperfections in the stone.

You'd weathered well, I thought: scarcely
an ounce of excess fat, still firm
just where you should be. My fingers sensed
no sagging in your flesh, no paper skin,
no ridging blood vessels. I felt

your heartbeat next to mine, could hear
your breathing find my rhythm, knew
for sure you were no statue. We stood
almost unmoving, let heat run through us,
warming our armature of ageing bone.

Lyn Moir

Shacking-up is Hard to Do

It takes some time to get it right,
for such old hands
we are surprisingly uncertain,
side-stepping each other
like that dance one does
on pavements with a stranger
or the nervous dithering
which ends up awkwardly
with me presenting the wrong cheek
to a proffered kiss – and it's not
the big or obvious differences
that make it tricky,
this last game of hide-and-seek –
not money, politics, religion,
sex – but the unexpected
and the junk that we've
brought with us
from our previous lives –
your preference for *café filtre,*
mine for Darjeeling, not Earl Grey,
the clutter which I love,
that statuette you hate,
the casual twisting of knives
in unhealed wounds,
the words we want to hear,
those we should leave unsaid
and which of us gets to sleep
on the window side of the bed.

Angela Kirby

In a Stateroom Without You

By now we'd be lying together, laughing
on this narrow berth, your fingers
in my silvered hair, your eyes
searching mine like a sailor's for land.
Our kisses would lengthen, deepen, not
skimming lips and necks.
Your body would fall onto mine
like fog on a dreaming village.
Beneath us, the ironed sheets would pleat,
the clothes dividing us thicken before
we cast them off. In my hands,
you'd become the wild, inevitable tide.

Instead, I'm here without you,
as one of us will almost surely be
after the other's death

our bodies separate, even after
years of embraces.
Yours is longer than mine,
your back strong as a keel, your hair
the murky gold of a certain seaweed

my breasts and belly mound like swells
my brown eyes crackle bright
as the moon on the waters.

No matter which body
will be without the other, both
will always be here

the way you're with me
in this stateroom: our bodies
always wherever fog
falls on the quiet cottages,
where tide is streaming
into the cracked and opening rocks –
after one body is left
then neither.

Mary Dingee Fillmore

Winter Love

Shall I still know you in your winter guise,
your thick hair white, your frame now brittle bones,
or shall I see you and not realise
this is my lover in his shrunken skin?
Some vague resemblance in your Baltic eyes
may strike a spark and laughter do the rest,
or blank incomprehension minimise
vibrations, mute the echoes of the past.
Or will your fingers, touching, recognise
my flesh in spite of mummifying time
which shrivels all? — though were that otherwise
there'd be no problem: you'd still be the same
and so would I. Perhaps we have the chance,
should we still wish, to get it right for once.

Lyn Moir

Metamorphobia

We celebrate the slub of ancient stone,
cracked, peeling bark, dog-back bristle,
the coarse embrace of linen homespun:
yet we fear etched faces,
gnarled hands and blemished limbs,
as if the only kind of nature we despise
is our own kind grown old.

Tell me, at what particular hour
do we become untouchable,
dulled negatives of ourselves,
unchanged in essence, but outwardly
rendered grotesque?
When does the prince change back into a frog?

The young do not want to know,
they cannot, they are too busy worshipping
the beautiful smooth faces mirrored
in their lovers' eyes to understand
that love does not cloud like a cataract,
the heart does not grow old.

This is the gift of years:
to see beneath the body's textured surfaces
the many layers of a steadfast life
laid down like sedimentary landscapes
imperceptibly;
and when, heroic in our vulnerability,
we kiss a swollen joint or fold of wilful flesh,
it's with a knowledge honed by mortality
to the tenderest edge.

Elisabeth Rowe

Letting Go

The Sod It Years

Here at last, the *sod it* years,
when *bugger it, why not?*
flies to the tongue
as quickly as chocolate cake.

In the years of *if not now then when?*
you might as well have it,
the dress or the fag or the man
or the bet on the nag.
You might as well grow it,
the spare tyre, the beard,
the hair in the ears.

Oh, the hell with it! Years
are such a relief: no more holding back.
Just do it, we say to an audience of one,
as the days turn to dust
and our bodies grow slack.
Who needs to be sober?
Who's looking at us?

Ann Alexander

105

Sometime Lately

Sometime lately I decided
to let myself slip. No longer
would I claim the title of
Good Cook. The relief was
instant and exquisite. No one
demands hospitality from
someone who burns stews,
serves overdone veg, forgets
how to cook sausages, vegetarian
naturally, and so on. It's not
such a crime. Now I don't
cook, I just assemble food
and hope for the best.

Sometime lately I realised
I could use this new slack
attitude in other areas of my life.
Transferable non-skills we could
call them. I could forget how
to polish my shoes or dust or
clean the bath every time.
I might just refuse to wear
make-up to gild the lily. Like it
or lump it I could say. Or have I
got past slack into rude? OK
I could even stop wearing knickers
when it's hot. I mean these days
who's to know, who's to look!

Sometime lately I felt
myself getting older and Time
slipping away so nowadays I'd
rather just have a sandwich
and read a book.

Berta Freistadt

106

Lieselott Among the Blackberries

Caught on September's
blackberry hook,
her hands reach out
for the sweet dark fruit;
wholly under
the blackberry spell.

'Hurry up, Lieselott,
it is late.' (Plenty
of time! She
feigns deaf and dawdles.)
Old woman tasting
the last of the fruit,
in sunny oblivion;
in a still brightness.

Gerda Mayer

If I Cannot

have first kisses again in the way
they only hint at what is possible
with slow tongues that are sleepy,
breathless with promise, and if I cannot
reclaim the first whisper of silk stockings,
of silk panties, the pulling on,
the sliding off and feel my hair all wild again,
snaking down my back, or set loose
in the breeze, tangled, unruly, startling
the face, taking it by surprise, from the front,
from behind, then I will settle for being
the crone poet – the famous crone poet.

I will want to recline on my velvet chaise,
to be Delphic, oracular, to dispense wisdom
with artful generosity, laced with innuendo,
to the crowd of sycophantic young bloods,
all smooth and articulate, who will gather
at my feet – especially the handsomest,
with their beckoning hands, their mouths
honeyed with admiration for my faded beauty,
my still-agile brain, murmuring sweetly,
moving closer in the evening workshop whirl,
their predatory clipboards tossed aside.

I will unlock my box of stored up fantasies
and scatter them like rose-petal confetti,
allowing the lads to bestow kisses on my hands,
regal and be-ringed, to stir the blood that still
pumps hot beneath the tissue paper skin.

I will want to feel their fresh lips on my
well-mapped cheeks, to open myself
to their insouciant patter, after the meal,
after the wine, after the creamy sweet,
and jeans – just a bit too tight, I will want
to savour the cool moisture of the last kiss
good night as it dries on my lips.

Wendy Klein

In the Mirror

You've launched no ships, inspired no work of art,
no princes abdicated thrones for you.
Seems age has withered you in every part
and custom staled, so nothing now is new.
But what a life you've had so far...   It shows
in knowing eyes. They've seen a lot, I guess.
Does wisdom always come as freshness goes?
You've earned each line, while every tooth – unless
your sight's kaput – appears much longer now.
Your crooked grin which once incited lust
still finds a lot to laugh at, anyhow.
I'll drink to you before you turn to dust,
dear duplicate. What if you've passed your peak?
There's value in each genuine antique.

Jenny Morris

Last Chance Saloon

'Set 'em up, kid' was your usual cry
as you sauntered through the door
with a look in your eye and a whisky sigh
and a voice that could sand the floor.

The girls in the back cleared out damn quick
for they knew that you were mine,
that anyone's try for a fuck on the fly
would put their life on the line;

and none of the guys, if they were wise,
would call for a beer or a shot
while you and I measured eye to eye,
never moving from the spot.

Now the tankards break as our clawed hands shake,
and our vision's none too clear,
but our eyes still meet though our fingers ache
and what the hell if the beer

is flat or the spirits drip as we sip,
there's no one in the bar,
and who bar us gives a tinker's cuss
if we spill the whole damn jar?

Those days were good, but these are fine,
we cuss, we kiss, and we drink good wine,
just thank the Lord for that, my dear,
thank the good Lord for that.

Lyn Moir

Real Estate Tango
Antibes

Remembering whistled cat-calls of warm-skinned Latins, lightly,
as into waltz-time or a slow foxtrot, I glide into flirtation,
an art to be savoured like that forgotten aphrodisiac, temptation.

I'm not daft – it's my euros not my baggy body he's after,
this turn-me-on, wink-to-win, forty-plus agent – but in the South,
dressed, undressed by sun, the years ripen a woman to autumnal

perfection. Tipsy on giggles, intent on buying *a proper view*,
I whirl about measuring views. We heel-turn and feather-step
on a medley of balconies while he displays his best apartments,

whisks tango in the blood, footwork super-smooth as he leads
in a swirl of link, stalk and pivot steps to the wild tempo
of a finale in which he swivels, spins, catches me – a done deal.

June Hall

Aquafit

November Friday mornings when the weather's
foul Glaswegian, see me out my bed
by half past nine, racing the traffic to Scotstoun.
I join the usual coven in the pool, ladies past
a certain age, warming up their tonsils.
Teacher arrives, cranks up the music machine,
and off we go, ready or not, to the sound of
'Running Bear', 'YMCA', Aga-doo-doo-doo.
At last, some use for those terrible songs
of our youth. Heads in various shades of
blonde bob along as we all run up to the
deep end, our lop-sided chests, diabetic legs,
plus plus sizes, varicose veins, paying
tribute to all the babies, the sweeties,
the drinks and fish suppers of our lives.
But here we are, out and proud, doing
frog jumps, star jumps, scissors jumps,
running up to the deep end, turning,
jumping backwards, turning.
'Turn, turn, turn,' she says, butter wouldn't melt.
Is she having a laugh? 'I'd like to turn her,'
someone remarks sourly. Giggles erupt.
'Get a woggle,' she shouts, as we all
tread water and those at the back of the class
return to the real business of the morning,
yackety-yack. Sometimes a man drifts across
by mistake, looking for the speed lane, not sure
what's going on, but we're oblivious (almost)
...give us a man after midnight and we're away,
heads bobbing again as we all kick in unison.
Teacher cracks the whip. 'Faster, kick those
legs – let me see knees, knees, knees!'

Someone says: 'Catch yer grannie daeing
this, eh?' We're all having a laugh, now,
some lewd joke or other, I can't catch it but
laugh anyway, and it's onto the last stretch,
little jumps, one, two, three, four, and jump
in the air, and 'Well Done' as we clap ourselves
and make our way, jelly-legged, to the showers,
all of us Dancing Queens fighting our Waterloo.

Rosemary McLeish

Exercising Preferences

Perhaps it's not too late
to learn to tango. As ankles creak
and weaken, ice-skating is out
although the yen to skim like
a stone across a lake is still strong.
Speleology was claustrophobic,
squash-balls sting
and abseiling causes panic.

I should be realistic,
set my sights on gentler activities
as muscles nowadays are less elastic
but yoga? or Pilates?

No! It's time to zip on the red satin
and go Latin.

Gill Learner

I am becoming my grandmother...

Sooner or later, in the great scheme of things,
Women are ambushed by their transformation
Into their own mothers. Mirrors tell them,
Or echoes of some little tetchiness
That still itches under skin that has thinned
To let it out again.

Not I;
I have skipped a generation and will soon
Become my grandmother. It has begun.
No longer can I pass a crying child
Without wiping its nose on my pinny
Or any dog without extending my hand.

I find all kinds of treasures in the street
And take them home with me in a string bag.
I touch flowers, move snails out of the way
Of passing traffic. All these things I do
Regardless of the present company.

The transformation has not gone unnoticed;
Somebody left a hurt newt in a bowl
Outside my door, convinced that I could help it.

And now, like her, I am the world's Aunt Jessie;
Old, fat and ugly, but – hurrah! God loves me!
Daily I hit the road in shapeless lace-ups
Dap-slapping my way across East Anglia,

Now and then turning my face up to heaven
Like a tanned leather bottle full of questions
To diagnose the illness of the wind
And look for little ways to make it better.

Ann Drysdale

'How nimble the old are'

How nimble the old are, balancing
as the world gyrates beneath them fast   faster
All that's familiar sweeps from touch
till their bones are honeycomb

You can't know how deftly I'm spinning
or how I love anything that hesitates
pauses sticks with me a minute
touches my flying head   Look

I've gathered a little parchment leaf
It settled against my cheek as damp and cool
as a child's kiss   We have happened
together   We slip away

M R Peacocke

Listing

Because I have acquired the rarity value
that comes with a long history,

because I am corrugated
with a fine grey patina –

The Society for the Conservation
of Rundown English Women (SCREW)
is attempting to have me listed.

They consider my mossy overhang,
my bulging sides,
to be ripe for preservation.
They admire the sturdy way
I have endured so many storms.

They fear that someone else
with doubtful taste
will turn up, take me over,
insist on radical dentistry,
Brazilian waxing, nip and tuck.
Atkins. Botox. Even a boob job.
And all the charm of a certain antique style
of woman would be lost.

Now I have been offered
to the National Trust.
Sightseers crowd my door,
curious to see what happens when
a woman simply grows old.

Ann Alexander

Ode to My Legs

These are the legs that launched
a thousand mini-skirts.
Girlfriend, look at them now.
These poor old pins, old lady
thunder-thighs as full of lumps
as turned soil, cellulose city
pocked and pitted like craters
on the moon. Thighs the size
of redwoods, knees swelling
to the heft of housemaids' bums;
flesh-eaters chomping at the shins,
paper-thin skin sloughing off
at the slightest sight of the sun,
not to mention ankles disappearing
behind pouches like dormice cheeks
hoarding stagnant water for a drought.

Never mind, they can still
put their feet up, potatoes on couches,
they can still walk (not on stilettos,
but camouflaged on beaches),
and once in a while, given
a following wind and a firm hand
on the tiller, they can trip
the light fantastic as gaily as
the girl in her hotpants and heels.

Rosemary McLeish

Observing My Future

I study the curve of my waist in the glass,
note how my weight is settling on my hips,
my thighs rounding nicely under them,
my flat feet splaying out.

You would see a woman ageing, *you'd*
attribute my appearance to
a shrinking of the spine,
too little exercise.

Ha! Don't you know how mirrors fib?
I see the mermaid lurking there,
I sense the hardening of my feet,
the scaling up of skin.

I wonder will I learn to sing
like wind inside a shell?
And when at last I spawn –
my hips so wide, so full –
what is it will emerge?

Gill McEvoy

Going Back

This seaside ballroom's where the dance-band played
below glass chandeliers and arching palms
where hearts could trip as hopes could be betrayed
and lust might turn to love in strangers' arms.

Now plaster cherubs on the ceiling smile
with broken lips to see the scene below.
A passing lame old girl can't reconcile
this empty night with those of long ago.

She hears faint melodies, remembers when
this was the most exciting place in town.
She whirled in gauze along the ranks of men.
But now all's derelict and falling down.

In this sad place of lost desire and chance
in darkness, by herself, she starts to dance.

Jenny Morris

Talking to Strangers

I've started doing it
now that I'm older with nothing to lose by way of pride,
virginity etcetera.

My mother did it,
in her breathless, indiscriminate need to be loved,
to make connections.

My father did it
embracing the dotty diversity of human nature with
curious compassion.

Children do it
beguiled by wicked fairies, witches, queens and wolves
and nice policemen.

Adolescents do it
adrift in a virtual world of chit-chat fantasy hungry for
instant romance.

And I've started doing it
in railway carriages and cafes (don't tell my daughter)
and it's amazing

how intimate you
can become with a complete stranger when you've
nothing to lose.

There's a man near the hospital resting his hands on a cane:
he's in textiles, his daughter's expecting a baby.
I tell him my newborn grandchild has Downs Syndrome,
and we share our loves, our fears, our vulnerability.

Outside the Italian food shop there's a woman drinking coffee.
She invites me back to show me photographs of her childhood
on the Isle of Man (the awful frumpy clothes we wore then)
and a girl called Judy who was in my class at boarding school.

On the train I'm next to a woman wearing a yellow T-shirt
that clashes with her yellow hair; she keeps on shushing
her child, and I want to tell her to avoid that particular colour
and let the child make a noise but I manage to keep quiet.

I must stop doing it:
I can see I shall get into trouble, even though I am older
with nothing to lose.

Elisabeth Rowe

Found It

I was unblocking the drain
with a shovel and a shove and a bucket of bleach
when I rediscovered my feminine side.

I remember the day I lost it,
after the birth of my second child
and before my first divorce.

My children ached to see it,
but it ran from us like money and love –
though sometimes we caught a glimpse.

And now it's back. Dated, dented,
dusty, doleful, demanding, distracted,
and definitely female.

I am old now, and have no more use for it.
I am old, and cannot afford the upkeep.
I will give it to my daughter. She will know
exactly what to do with it.

Ann Alexander

The Missing

Friends
i.m. Maureen and Jeanne

I want to be sure I'll never forget
their voices. One came from Manchester
and her speech was like my grandma's.
Her tone was pleasantly low for a woman,
warm, often full of laughter, and rich
from knowing its owner's mind. The other
spoke with a gentle, reassuring resonance.
Hers was a trained, actress's voice, yet so
sincere I could confess all
my fears to it, and all my hopes.

In my head I repeat things they said:
'I'll come in the spring.' But she didn't come.
'I miss you, Jan.' But I didn't visit.
Regrets and guilt. Friends are precious.
They and I grow old. These two died this year.
It's April and the cherry blossom's out.

Janet Loverseed

Returning Veva

We arrived early to locate the once familiar grave,
its earth, once tamped from footsteps and fresh flowers,
careless now among sheathed arums
and grass, lush
and thick, springing back against our threshing sticks.

We scattered the mother's dust over her child's grave,
her life, once stamped with kaleidoscopic hours,
silent now under crusted lichen
and snails, ashed
and grey, burnt bones swirling with blossoms of May.

Ruth O'Callaghan

Slipping Away
i.m. Rosemary Varney

Slipping one morning so uncharacteristically
away, you left without explanation, nor –
stranger still – have sent word later, not even a
sardonic comment on what you found there (wherever
that is). Where is your laugh? the calling
horn of your voice?

And where, now, can we find you? I've looked
everywhere. The garden is empty except of
snowdrops (you planted them) and in the kitchen
stand bowls and cups you made, but aren't using
today, again. Your books lean together, or open
at poetry that I've not heard you quote
for days. And you haven't hidden mischievously
in the wardrobe, though it trails your glowing
rusts and oranges from swinging hangers.

At night I see you disjointedly in strange
houses or streets, only in the morning
returning to absence. You haven't spoken now
for over a week. I keep expecting to see
your prow of a nose forging through the winter
air, to put my arms round your frailness and
then be startled by the sharp relish of
your latest saying.
                    But you've found
a new way to surprise me.

Christine Webb

Why didn't you tell me you were dead?

It was odd the way I found out:
coming across your name
on a plaque on that bench
(in Roman caps. HE LOVED THIS VIEW)

I thought of you –
never one to commend any view –
rebellious, cranky, funny;
touching my life then losing touch.

The years wound back
to you, leaning forward
either to kiss or to mock;
your beard vibrant with intent.

Not a bad idea, these markers
we invent, stretching our time
that single heartbeat more,
cairns, gravestones, pyramids,
plaques, words written
on a dark and shifting floor.

Connie Bensley

Encounter

They walk along the road. She,
her white hair neatly cut,
a fringe framing her lively face;
he rather bald on top, short back and sides
sometimes in comfortable silence,
in animated talk at other times;
an ordinary couple
walking hand in hand.

And I think: Damn them, damn them,
must they stir up once more
what should be long forgotten, laid to rest;
the anguish, pain, reproach
that you have left me,
that you are at a place that never
lets anyone come back,
while they, like we before,
are walking hand in hand.

Alice Beer

Seven Weeks

Seven weeks today. A July wind
is tousling the trees, rumpling the garden.
I have written five letters, washed the sheets.
A mistake somewhere – I've not finished
the crossword. Sit with the sounds of Sunday.
Thrashing leaves. Cows. Planes. My own breath.

All week the air has burnt: it is breath
from a lion's mouth. No stir of wind
to brush the cheeks of the sixth Sunday:
silence quivers in the house, and the garden,
shrivels, as if the season's finished.
I sort bed linen. There are too many sheets.

A week leafed with letters. I scan these sheets
about you, half alert to hear your breath
until the words remind me that it's finished.
So sorry to hear. Rain in the wind
hasn't enough weight to nourish the garden.
Bells clang dryly. It is the fifth Sunday.

I wake in your presence the fourth Sunday –
not lying passive between your sheets
but laughing, striding in the summer garden,
your mouth full of kisses, and your breath
sweeter and stronger than the June wind.
Why did I wake before the dream was finished?

Ready to go. *I've nothing left unfinished*
you told me once. But now beside a Sunday
river I want you here to watch the wind
curving sails, to feel the hauled sheets
as the boats put about, to taste the breath
of summer gusting down from every garden.

The second week I meet you in the garden
sitting under the oak where you once finished
fixing the swing-seat; not out of breath
but quiet and absorbed, reading the Sunday
papers, glancing up, rustling the sheets,
pinning one down that flutters in the wind.

I look out at the garden that first Sunday
when everything is finished. I smooth the sheets
and listen for your breath. There is only the wind.

Christine Webb

Thumbs Down

nearly forty years and now after such
a short time bits of you are fading away

I remember them in words
but I've mislaid the pictures

the puzzlement above your eyebrows
every time you asked what *is* perfect pitch?

that crimp of skin on your back
where you had to have a cyst removed

the mild and fleeting gleam in your eye
when your logic got the better of me

and now your hands, your hands
not beautiful, not elegant, but kind

and I can't remember the set of your thumbs
how stupid   I've lost your thumbs

Gina Shaw

Gold is Lonely

when the moon gilds patterns
on the stillness of the sea

when a field of buttercups
a million goblets of sungleam
is a memory we shared

when light glints glory
on a girl's red-blonde hair

when the yellow rose
you planted for me
in the garden that we made
springs leaves

when three continents
return a family
to mourn
our golden anniversary

Bernie Kenny

Roses for Remembrance

Dear Lord,
You will have found by now
how irritating Jim can be.
I bet You've heard the parrot joke
some twenty-seven times
and still don't think it's funny.
So although You are perfection
I am sure You will agree that there are days
when murder seems a reasonable act.
Take our trips to Tesco –
three times a week since we retired.
Jim would always drive.
'No need to rush,' he'd say,
(forgetting that I'd washing on
or scones to bake for tea).
'There's lots to see along the way.
My! Mrs Phillip's roses are a treat.'
He'd say it every time till I was fit to scream.
You'll have noticed the annoying way
he keeps repeating things.

Dear Lord,
I go to Tesco now alone,
driving in our strangely empty car.
But when I pass that splash of floribunda
within my head once more I hear Jim's voice.
'My! Mrs Phillip's roses are a treat.'

So Lord, if you can spare the time
from war and want and pestilence,
please give a thought to Mrs Phillip's roses
and keep them aphid free.

Margaret Wood

Delivery from the 'Crem'

The wooden box was passably presented;
It was the bag inside that made me cry.
The stapled see-through plastic I resented,
Although the box was passably presented –
You'd think the wit of man could have invented
Something more suited to a fond goodbye.
The box itself was passably presented.
It was the bag inside that made me cry.

Ann Drysdale

Feeding the Ducks at Calstock

This was one of the places we had shared.
I had imagined I would be alone;
The place was packed with grockles. I was scared
To make much ceremony on my own.
The smell of chips lay heavy on the air,
The day was hot, the Tamar brown and thick.
I needed to complete my business there
And felt it would be best if I were quick:
Off with the lid, a surreptitious fling.
A cloud of spinning bits sank in the murk
And, terrified of missing anything,
All the assembled wildfowl went berserk.
Feeding the ducks? I heard somebody say.
Something like that, I said, and turned away.

Ann Drysdale

This Morning

we were there, in our walled back garden,
and you, my love, picked a few coxes off the tree
which puzzled me because we never had an apple tree
and even as I thought this you were gone, so I
went through the back door into the kitchen
with its red quarry-tiled floor and
the blue and white check curtains, the sink
under the window, the saucepans upside down
on the shelf opposite, the mug tree
with its blue and white mugs on the cupboard
next to the draining board as usual so I wondered
what the young man, reminding me of you
was doing in the kitchen with his arms
round a laughing young woman, when I woke
and remembered it was more than eighteen years
since I moved to my sunny little flat
overlooking the square.

Alice Beer

Amnesty

I burned your coat in November,
Bonfire Night, when else?
God knows, that coat was you:
stubborn in the way it wouldn't burn,
awkward in the way it slumped on top the pile,
out of shape with everything,
the world, itself.

That coat was every morning
when I couldn't start the day on time:
you to wash and dress, kids to get to school,
and you, soiled again: three more lines
of washing, sheets, pyjamas, towels
to hang outside.

That coat was each Day Centre afternoon
when you refused to get in the car and I,
with murder in my heart – shopping to fetch,
washing to bring in before the rain,
dinner burning slowly on the stove –
would force you in, all sixteen stone,
then feel the scald of tears.

It played a last trick when it burned:
a button loosed by flame fell from the fire,
rolled to rest at my right foot. It lay there
like a small dog begging amnesty.
Next morning when I raked the ashes flat
I picked it up. Now it goes
everywhere with me.

Gill McEvoy

A Break in the Clouds

blue sky after rain
I patrol the garden

the grass which looked dead
has jumped up plump and juicy

the skinny clematis I thought was dying
has run to the top of the fence and flowered

then a movement – petals
dropping from the red rose

and I realise I haven't
thought of you for minutes

Gina Shaw

Burly

The big man rows out to a place
where we can hardly see him.

Frail as a leaf now, he assumes
the position of a horizon.

He causes us to look often.
We cannot resist turning our heads.

See where the wake widens out to touch us,
where our footprints subside.

His eyes were like warm metal.
He was the ballast.

So many footprints now.
The winter sun is on our backs.

A cold wind has been blowing for weeks.
How we've stooped.

How we've bent to the contours of loss.
It astonishes us how easily

we make room for it, how willingly
we adjust. Like a womb or a cave.

It fits perfectly inside the rib cage.
How strong and burly grief is.

Pat Winslow

Nearly There?

The Fallers

We are the fallers, cradling
bruises and broken wrists
as the skin around our eyes
turns purple, then yellow –
we are the confused,
the nuisances,
the grumblers, the shufflers
in downtrodden slippers
and stained dressing-gowns,
those for whom doctors
and nurses have little time,
they prefer the biddable –
who lie here, neat and quiet
between their clean sheets
and hospital-corners,
who put up with things,
do not complain,
who have patient smiles,
and do not, like us,
disturb the docile, wet
their beds, ring their bells,
cry out *Nurse, Nurse, Nurse* –
or howl at midnight.

Angela Kirby

No Joke, Growing Old

Funny how we wrinklies shrink into
a cartoon version of ourselves,
grinning and giggling, eyes a pop,
scribble of hair all anyhow or not at all.

Each day a red nose day, although
we hardly know what year it is,
blinking at The Sun.

I say I say I say (cue laughter) hey!
I used to be, I used to know, I used to live –
yeah, right!

Heard the one
about the bandy legged geezers
in their ankle flapping pants
and kipper ties, skidding
on the day's banana skin
from sparrow fart to nighty-night?
Have you seen us oops-a-daisy grannies
daubing lipstick on frayed smiles?
Two sherries and we're tight.

Toodle pip! All a bit of fun.
A target now for every tittering rogue.
A hoot, a scream, a fright.

After lunch the noisy, open-mouthed
post-prandial; then a g&t or two

before we climb the wooden hill
to kip, warbling an antique song.
Too bad we always spoil the joke
by going on too long.

Ann Alexander

Protest

Is the rebellion that's taking place
against malnourishment or overwork?
Where phalange and metacarpal interlock,
fluids have dried or minerals collected.
Fingers still show willing on the keys
but maybe they're about to go on strike.

I used to press the joints to hear
a kindling-snap. Mum said that I'd regret it
one fine day. But it's the rainy ones
that light a fire near where the pen-shaft rests,
when the wrist recalls a teenage sprain,
a thumb resurrects a dislocating fall.

If all this was smouldering and I didn't know
until a month or so ago, what else is happening?

Gill Learner

Hang On, Mr Prufrock

I have measured out my life with coffee spoons
TS Eliot

It's not the spoons
but too much inherited linen, extra beds
except at Christmas and summer.

It's not the spoons but successions
of photographs, ageing in silver frames.
And too few places laid at the table.

Time is a breaker surging towards me.
High stepping, I try to resist the suck of the sand.
To keep balance, not drift, jelly-legged
to the sea bed, sooner.

I measure the walk on the high ridge,
the sound of the surfer's sail,
the new-planted cherry.

The painted interior, lit on the wall in sunset scarlet.
The gleam on the bronze, the dancing mote on the ceiling.
The ladder of light in the morning hall.

This is the measuring
I do, for dear life.

Josie Walsh

Life Work

Grey days spread mosses, Lilliputian
ropes over muscle and bone.

She reads the geology under each
visitor's smile,
aware they perceive her eroded,
aged, frail,
forget the lines
on her skin have netted life.

She has inner topography;
charts and maps
for places where she found treasure,
family skeins,
embroidery of friendships,
networks, distillations,
artefacts made from clunch of love.

Cave paintings
she alone accomplished,
rich in ochre, umber, heliotrope.

Isobel Thrilling

Stile

It leans the wrong way, tipped into the hill,
grey oak, worn, mis-angled for climbing –
or for rest. Rooted in soil slip it's out of true
like me. I scramble up, shaky from the climb,

perch off-centre on its disobliging frame
and through a tunnel of hips and hazels
watch the valley roll into shadow,
a reminder of the downhill trek ahead.

Gone are my hurtling days
of whoop and bound through thistle fields.
Side steps slide and fumble, nervous of mud
squelched deep by cattle hooves.

The last stile to the road is new,
solid, clean-grained, glowing amber,
paired with a shiny aluminium gate
whose easy swing, unlatched, surprises me.

June Hall

Woodlouse

has scaled half-way up
the Everest of my stair carpet
riser   tread   riser   tread

I've gone up noticing him
forgotten my purpose
come back down to find

him at the bottom
bumbling about like me
lost   looking for
                     something

Gina Shaw

Evensong

And then, and then the words returned
like the round wafer pressed into my hand
to make the way straight and the rough place plain
but red, still red, the colour of recognition.

To fossick should yield surprises. Seldom does.
But fumbling through unwanted fog, I stop
because a single call shows me kokako here again
bathing, drinking (at the lowest water trough)

along the track that winds round Wattle Valley.
Not blue, not black, but something in between,
the family Callaeidae, blue-wattled crows
call again three organ notes, each to the other

and this is not, not now, was once, a life ago but
present in the imprinted gift, in that part of memory
which keeps, under its own random key, the miracles
playing between bad dreams, where names have fled

and slipped into their cavities: surnames, names of streets
and squares, of authors, times, and where I put my purse.
It is the labels that I lose. The picture of the purse,
the smell, sounds, sight of rare birds bathing all remain.

Hilary Elfick

Puzzle

Look – here's my mind working –
a duplicate in a jar on the desk.
I'm shocked by the wear and tear.
The grooves it has and the false colours,
the slouch and tilt of it,
the splits, badly stitched,
and, heavens, the lurid light it works in –

how can I see what's out there
through a lens so curved,

how focus through a scope
so practised at peering back?

Pamela Coren

On Growing Old

Like mice in the night
the years that pass are gnawing
at our life ahead.

Bit by bit the paths
our life takes seem narrower,
steeper and more rugged.

The ruts get deeper,
the woods more dense, the bright star
before us brighter.

Alice Beer

Thrift

Sometimes you see them in a promenade shelter
sitting bolt upright, always facing the pier.
His thumb makes small circles

on the swollen knuckles of her hand.
Or perhaps it's she who wipes custard
from the faint rasp of his chin,

as he sits in the taint of clothes communally
washed and the penetrating ghost of pee.
They're hoarders. They know how

to make a very little go a long way.
The faint quiver of shadow
at the corner

of her mouth may mean 'smile'
and the twitch of his eyelid
could signify 'wink'.

Pity is too easy, as they repeat
in their various permutations of grey
the road sign, Elderly People Crossing,

for they have learned thrift. How to weigh
out each tiny gesture towards the other,
how you translate a long silence

into the currency of kindness.
Their sort of love is tough as a Kevlar vest.
They lay out the last ounce cannily, on care,

making it last.
Shouldn't we start practising now
for that tender paradigm shift from words to touch?

Kate Foley

Running

Once there was running, a spurt of joy
in the feet, unbidden, some riot
under the skin.
Later there was running, willed.
Now the body's dull
like the lips of grazing animals
mumbling at frozen grass. If I say,
Do you remember running?
It pauses, puzzled. It has its tasks.
It can't recall.

M R Peacocke

The Years

They cuckooed their way into my flimsy nest,
trampled bluebells in the smoky beech woods,
lolled at trestle tables under the tulip tree,
and told me summer would never end.
They bled the crimson hawthorn, stripped the sloe
and breathed hoar frost on every twig
and seed-head – subtler, more beautiful
than morning's beaded webs – and then
they vanished, leaving sunsets to die for.

Elisabeth Rowe

On the Way Down

An old ewe kesent among rushes, lodged
belly up in her blanket of dirty fleece,
cleft stare fixed on dying.

Our fists clenching deep into ragged wool
couldn't haul her up to rights. Only her fear
buckled her back to life

and sent her lurching from the smell of us
and the alien voices, out of our hands,
till at last she settled

to the sweet rummage of grass. Months, perhaps,
maybe a spring to nourish a spindling lamb.
So we took on the fleece

of doubtful weather, looking back at times,
and followed the harsh track down. One more season?
We are making old bones.

M R Peacocke

The Blue Armchair

They tell me I'm too old to live alone
For years home has been here, where
steps climb down to my four rooms,
not grand but infinitely dear,
walls of local granite, terrace garden,
window framing Dalkey Sound,
and I am owner of it all.

Never to see my ordinary things
in their accustomed place,
 the blues I've chosen for this room,
my father's set of Dickens
among the rows of books,
friends round the table,
absence in a blue armchair

Bernie Kenny

Selling Up

The last are gone. I have called up
the yellow heifers from the field
with their coats crisp against winter
and sold them away. It is gain and loss.
Their absence is like a fasting.

This morning a rainbow planted
its shaft full into the cropped grass
and I thought foolishly of Noah
alone in the ark, an empty bucket
in his hand and nothing to do,

and wondered what he would have missed
the most, hay smells or slop and steam
of dung, or the way the old cow
could speak under her breath to the new calf,
or a curled yellow poll to scratch.

M R Peacocke

Departure Lounge

Still It Ain't Over

We have taken the last card from the pack,
laid down the losing hand,
considered last month's stars
that failed to warn us of
the creek we now drift into.

And still it ain't over.

We are all through considering
the runes, the cast die, the way the sticks fall,
eating the crumbled cookies,
digesting the hat.
The cup has arrived at the lip.
The many slips and the hatched chicks
have all been counted. And still.

Nothing for it
but to uncross our fingers, ditch
the rabbit's foot, walk under ladders,
kick the black cat, send for the fat lady,
say boo to a goose.

Ann Alexander

Age

We should turn gold
with age
like leaves,
decay into the colours
of antiquity
in the manner of rocks
and sunsets.

Life long-distilled
should thin
in a wineglass of bone,
vintage summers
fermenting inner fire;
a hint of ice.

Death would come quiet
as snow,
creating a landscape
mythical with frost
where trees break into
silver thorn;
configurations of spring.

Isobel Thrilling

The Right Bones

'Where do birds usually go to die?' you ask
'Is there somewhere like an elephants' graveyard?'

A passing car or cat got this one.
Its down jacket must still be warm.

Quills are oil-slick bright, upstanding
but its ruby eyes are dull little gravels

and its coral feet a crippled grey.
Somebody, imitating the reticent

decency of the way birds like to die,
has swept it into a doorway.

I imagine a bird feeling its pulse fail,
settling its last warmth

on the I Ching puzzle of its ancestors' bones
folding the wings it won't need

round the small leaves of its feet,
quietly letting the migratory knot

in its forehead fade.
I would like that too

one day
if only I can find the right bones.

Kate Foley

Celebration

The years are stretching
her yarn, used and re-used.
Her cloth, more in tune
with the weave.

She watches the young
spinning their newness.
Her love pattern spreads
over table and feast.

Her shawl in the wind,
when deep colour fades,
like the mat of a nomad
she'll roll up her life.

Josie Walsh

A Very Private Conversation

Surrounded by a summer sea of sky
and as many shades of green
as years of history,
I am content
to lie back on this fringed scarp
and speak to a god.

I tell him that here,
in the crooked arm of the valley,
quiet with grasshoppers and curlew,
the trattle of quaking grass,
I'm unafraid of the past
weighted with death,
unafraid of dying here,
how I hope the crows

will profit from my flesh
and leave my bones
gleaming in chalk and flint;
that I could invite death
to come now
but how
I will not write this poem
until tomorrow.

Pat Borthwick

You Go Your Way

Cremation, you say. You'd rather
burn than end up in a box
in the earth. Supposing, just when
the gravedigger has tamped down
the last spadeful and started
to walk away, you suddenly
take another breath, too late:
you'll suffocate.

Burial, I say. Better by far
to go six feet below than burn.
Supposing, just when the attendant
has clanged shut the incinerator
and lit the gas, I suddenly shudder
back to life, hearing my bones crack.
Rather than know that sound
I'll go cold underground.

Gina Shaw

Save Your Breath

Faint last words waver up
from hospital pillows:

You will look after Jack won't you?
He needs combing for fleas morning and evening.

For God's sake make sure you pay off your mortgage
before you go skiving off to Goa;

And Angela, you must give up that dreadful man
he's no good for you at all.

The relatives nod and nod, leaning forward tenderly,
their fingers crossed behind their backs.

Connie Bensley

Nanny Besom

There were witches when I was young.
Sometimes a light surprises   Door
cracks open   A solid figure
flits.   Is it you, Nanny Besom?

Taint of breath. Fingers pruned to pinch.
And let me see your tongue   Have we
been a good girl and have we been?
Whisking away my tears like crumbs.

Such scouring syrups. Nanny's eyes
are measuring spoons. Her barbed chin
trembles towards a north of guilt.
In winter, in the grey of it,

in the tallow sun, when sometimes
my heart's cold swells like ice in pipes
and I suffer a dull fraying
and uncoupling of life from hope,

she visits, a tarnished spirit.
In she slips, treading knuckled ground,
unwinding from her bag the death
I fear, unloving, clinical.

M R Peacocke

Going Light

They call it 'going light', the loss of substance
That goes with the failing of the spirit
When the end comes.

My old dog went light just before he died.
His thin bones whispered in his hairy skin
And went to sleep

And all that was left of him was the light
That faded slowly as his eyes went dim;
The other light.

Going light, light going. It was as if
I had perceived a sort of sense in it
For a moment.

Two kinds of light, making an hourglass
Laid on its side between weight and darkness;
The shape of dying.

Death is the snapping of the narrow neck
In between substance and oblivion
And that is all.

And as you come near to the glass isthmus
I wish for the breaking to be gentle.
Go light, my love.

Ann Drysdale

Mr Irresistible

So it's come to this,
I hang about all day, wasting
my time, wait for you,
whisper your name, shiver
at the thought of your caresses
until at last you swagger in,
late and shameless, making
one of your brief appearances
and staking out your claim.

Worse, I confess this too –
I sleep badly now, dreaming
of you throughout the night,
you and those ambiguous,
half-cold embraces of yours
which make me sweat and tremble.

I trace your finger's touches
on my skin, so light, so gentle,
yet see how they've left me
webbed over with fine lines.

I lick the sticky, barely-
perceptible smears
with which you streak
and mark me as your own,
I taste the stains
that cling like faded bruises.

How arrogant you are,
how well, how quickly
you have come to know me,
yet sometimes, even now
at this last hour, I hesitate,
drawing back, afraid.

But what do you care?
Indifferent, sure of yourself,
you wander off and disappear
for a while, aware that few
can deny you for long.

Ultimately, you will not take no
for an answer, persistent,
irresistible Death, my last
and only faithful lover.
I swear it,
I'll burn for you yet.

Angela Kirby

The Birthright

Death is your birthright, guard it well.
(In these days, even death's uncertain.)
Some Clever-Dick could put the hurt on
Eternally – which would be hell.

Seventy-seven years should serve
For feats of love, for feasts of blood:
For wickedness, for doing good,
Death is no more than we deserve.

Gerda Mayer

I Have Looked on the Faces of the Dead

They do not sleep, they are not
just in the next room,
they have not passed peacefully
on before, they are gone,
clearly and terribly,
with no comfort to be had
in them – even before
they were put in the earth
they were lost to me.

If they are anywhere, my mother,
my child, my three brothers,
my friend Nina, my lovers,
they have not let me know,
there have been no messages,
nor rapping on tables.

and if, occasionally, I feel
one or other of them to be
near me for a while, it is only
in much the same way
I imagine at times
to be in the presence of God,
think that I have been
somewhere before,

know what lies round
the next corner, what someone
is about to say – or that you
will telephone – and I remind
myself that scientists can give

rational explanations
for all such things –
which is more than can be said
for any of the churches.

Angela Kirby

170

Breaking Glass

Against the gathering
crowd of backs I hear
the dreadful sound of earth
on wood knock knocking
on that solid door knock knocking
wondering if you're there.

The worm winds slowly round
of people in their sober best this
final act to say farewell as earth
flies soft complicit deep
I cannot do I stand and weep.

Berta Freistadt

You Know it will Happen

even as you're laying out celery on the chopping board,
or slicing bread or emptying a tin of beans into a pan,
when you're lighting the gas or reading a book, having a pee,
watching TV. You could be on the phone or winding down
the window to look at a view. You could be farting, you could
be laughing or reading the paper. You could be cycling to work
or opening a letter. Or swimming, sunbathing, having sex.
You could be at the vet's or waving to a neighbour, or half-way
up a ladder painting the ceiling. Or even reading this poem.
It could happen and there'd be nothing you could do.

Pat Winslow

Order With Confidence

You have been specially selected to receive
our innovative Catalogue of Deaths.
Order with confidence from our unique
and quality-assured collection!

On special offer this week is Sudden Death,
for those who have set their affairs in order
and don't like saying goodbye.
Satisfied customer Mr. X drove smack into
the back of a van on the M 62.

For the less adventurous we recommend
our Default Death, the long slow gathering
of aches and pains that wear you out in the end.

Impress your friends with our attractive
personalised Home Death: go in your own bed,
with pets, family etc. around you
(last supper and last rites optional).

Should medical attention be required,
we have a special Hospital Package:
choose between standard and foundation status
and specify resuscitation frequency.

For an extra monthly premium we can guarantee you
a Hospice Death among cheery volunteers
with all the latest advances in palliative care.

Please note: we are not licensed for euthanasia
but single tickets to The Netherlands are available
from our travel section. Those interested in suicide
should consult the relevant web-sites.

We regret we cannot offer a service to those little ones
for whom the bell rings at the end of playtime.

Elisabeth Rowe

A Different Ceremony

Rusted root of darkness, branched artery of rock,
black as the fire-hardened tip of a throwing spear.

Bison dance a thunderous jig,
stately as a mountain falling.

Dumb as the quiet mouths of baby girls
littered on hillsides, death tries

with all its mimetic powers to show
that falling is not done to the leaf –

it knows best how. If we could trust
that weightless fall through air, clear

as the good stream that carries us anyway,
not answerable to stop or go,

then Theseus could swing the Minotaur into a waltz
and the ceremonies of death might be different.

Kate Foley

Coda

The Old Women and the Sea

What is it about old women and the sea?
But wherever there is a secluded cove
Or an inviting bit of sand
There are the women,
Many with a million wrinkles,
Gracefully accepting their due from the sun,
Giving their bodies to the water.

Once, when they were young, it dandled them;
Now their limbs carve it, they sculpt it
Into shapes of their fantasy,
The sea their atelier,
Their oeuvre, created
Year after painstaking year, with the blades of their limbs:
The slope of a shoulder, hollow of a thigh,
The calm, long focus of their gaze,
The grace in the fall of a hand.

Hermione Sandall

175

The Poets

Ann Alexander's collections from Peterloo are *Facing Demons* (2002) and *Nasty, British & Short* (2007). She won first prize in Mslexia's poetry competition (2007), the Frogmore Prize (2000), and Bedford Open (2007), and second prize in BBC's Poem for Britain. She is married, with one daughter, and lives in Cornwall.

Alice Beer was born and educated in Vienna, where she studied psychology and English. She came to England in 1937 and stayed because of Hitler. Widowed, with three children, she started writing poems in her seventies. Widely published in magazines and anthologies, she has two collections: *Facing Forward, Looking Back* and *Talking of Pots, People and Points of View*.

Connie Bensley lives in London and the most recent of her six poetry collections is *Private Pleasures* (Bloodaxe Books 2007). She was a prizewinner in the Tate Gallery and Observer competitions and was on the judging panel for the Forward Prize in 2004.

Pat Borthwick lives in East Yorkshire. She has been writer in residence in many rural settings and has a reputation for running innovative creative writing workshops and giving sparkling readings. Pat has three full-length collections of poetry, her poems frequently appearing as prizewinners in prestigious competitions. She is a Hawthornden Fellow.

Carole Bromley teaches creative writing for York University. Her poems have been widely published in magazines and anthologies and she has won a number of competitions, including the Bridport. Twice a winner in the Poetry Business competition, she has two pamphlets from Smith/Doorstop, *Unscheduled Halt* (2005) and *Skylight* (2009).

A C Clarke has published *The Gallery on the Left* (Akros 2003) and *Breathing Each Other In* (Blinking Eye Press 2005), her first full collection. She was the Makar for the Federation of Writers (Scotland) for 2007–2008. Her second collection, *Messages of Change,* has just been published by Oversteps Books.

Christine Coleman writes poetry and fiction. Her pamphlet collection is *Single Travellers* (Flarestack 2004). As part of the poetry ensemble 'Late Shift', she has performed at literary festivals, including Edinburgh. For details of her novels, *The Dangerous Sports Euthanasia Society* and *Paper Lanterns*, read her blog 'Writing Matters' on www.christinecoleman.net.

Pamela Coren taught Medieval and Renaissance literature in the English department at Leicester until retiring in 2000 to concentrate on writing. She has since published in many magazines and won some prizes. Her first collection, *The Blackbird Inspector,* was published by Laurel Books in 2005. She lives in Stamford.

Ann Drysdale was born near Manchester, raised in London, married in Birmingham; she ran a smallholding and brought up three children in Yorkshire. She now lives in South Wales. Her four collections from Peterloo include *Between Dryden and Duffy* (2005). A fifth, *Quaintness and Other Offences,* is due out soon from Cinnamon Press.

Hilary Elfick has a background in teaching and broadcasting, and has published eleven books, including a novel. She performs regularly in Australia and New Zealand, as well as in Britain. She is a mother of three and grandmother of five and spends five months a year in NZ working in conservation.

Mary Dingee Fillmore earned her MFA at Vermont College after a twenty-five year career in organisational development and a hidden life as a writer. Her poetry, about the Holocaust in the Netherlands and other subjects appears in *Upstreet, Pearl, Diner, Westview, Main Street Rag, Pinyon* and *Blueline*; also online and in various anthologies.

Kate Foley was a midwife, then changed horses and became Head of English Heritage's Ancient Monuments Laboratory. She now lives in Amsterdam, where she is a poetry editor for *Versal*. She leads workshops and gives frequent readings in the UK, Holland and elsewhere. Her fourth collection is *The Silver Rembrandt* (Shoestring Press 2008).

Berta Freistadt, a prolific and popular poet, sadly died shortly before the publication of this book. Everyone who knew her is missing her vibrancy, her wit, her generosity of spirit. Her enormous courage in enduring a long series of illnesses with her indomitable humour intact remains a source of inspiration.

June Hall, former editor and literary agent, with children off at 'uni', is now thoroughly enjoying life after sixty in spite of Parkinson's. She published her first collection, *The Now of Snow* (2004), under the Belgrave Press imprint, and had such a great time doing it that *Bowing to Winter* is coming out the same way in February 2010.

Joy Howard has lived in West Yorkshire for over twenty years. Poetry has always been part of her life, and her work was frequently anthologised during the 1980s. After retirement in 2005, she returned to writing, and co-founded Grey Hen Press. She is having the time of her life.

Bernie Kenny lives in Dalkey, Co. Dublin. She is a retired teacher, a mother of six, and has been widowed for five years. She has published four collections – *Poulnabrone* (2002), *Progeny* (2004), *Isle of Thorns* (2006) and A *Walk in Dalkey* (2008) – and *Gone to Earth*, a book of poems translated from Irish.

Angela Kirby was born in Lancashire in 1932 and lives in London. She has five children and has been a chef, garden designer, journalist and author. Her poems are widely published and have been translated into Romanian. Shoestring Press published her first collection, *Mr. Irresistible,* in 2005, and her second, *Dirty Work*, in 2008.

Wendy Klein has had a good year with a prize in the Southport (2009) competition, followed by first prize in the Ware (2009) Competition. Her first collection, *Cuba in the Blood* (Cinnamon Press) came out in the same year. She is crossing her fingers her luck has not run out!

Gill Learner has been widely published in journals and anthologies, not least A *Twist of Malice* (Grey Hen 2008). Winner of a number of awards including the Poetry Society's Hamish Canham Prize 2008, she has two 'northern' grandchildren but lives in Reading where she reads with Brickwork Poets. See also www.poetrypf.co.uk/gilllearnerpage.

Dinah Livingstone has published nine pamphlets and seven books of her poetry, the latest being *Presence* (2003) and *Kindness* (2007) (Katabasis, London). She has also published prose books and translations of poetry and prose. She edits the magazine *Sofia* and has lived in Camden Town, London, since 1966.

Janet Loverseed is lucky to have two children, five grandchildren, and a partner who encourages her writing. She started getting her poems accepted by magazines in her fifties, and is this year the proud winner of the first Grey Hen Competition. Her pamphlet *The Under-ripe Banana* is published by HappenStance.

Alwyn Marriage's six books include poetry and non-fiction. She is a university lecturer, and also gives frequent guest lectures and poetry readings. She was previously chief executive of two international literacy and literature aid agencies and editor of a journal, and is now Managing Editor of Oversteps Books. See also www.marriages.me.uk.

Gerda Mayer was born in Czechoslovakia and came to England aged eleven. Collections from Chatto & Windus, Oxford University Press, Peterloo Poets, Iron Press etc. Her *Monkey on the Analyst's Couch* (Ceolfrith Press) was a Poetry Book Society recommendation. Her *Prague Winter* (autobiographical prose vignettes) was published by Hearing Eye.

Gill McEvoy is Artistic Director for 'Chester Oyez!' annual festival of the poetry, drama and storytelling. She runs regular events: ZEST! Open Floor Poetry, The Poem Shed workshop, The Golden Pear Poetry Reading group. Pamphlets: *Uncertain Days* (Happenstance, 2006) and *A Sampler* (Happenstance, 2008); *The Plucking Shed*, a first collection, due from Cinnamon in 2010.

Rosemary McLeish was born in 1945. She started developing her creative side when she was forty. She is an 'outsider' artist, making miniatures, painting, and working with textiles; she writes poetry, articles and stories. She lives in Glasgow with her husband and cats.

Lyn Moir, born in Scotland in 1934, has published collections with Arrowhead in 2001 and 2003. Her third, *Velazquez's Riddle*, is due from Bluechrome in 2009, as is a fourth, provisionally titled *Easterly Force 10*, from Calder Wood Press. A Hawthornden fellow, she lives in St. Andrews.

Jenny Morris writes poems and fiction. She travelled and had forty different addresses before she reached the age of forty. Her writing has won awards and appeared in many magazines and anthologies (including *A Twist of Malice*). Her latest poetry collection is *Lunatic Moon*.

Ruth O'Callaghan, a Hawthornden Fellow, competition adjudicator, interviewer and reviewer, hosts two London poetry venues. Awarded an Arts Council grant, she visited Mongolia to collaborate with women poets. Her first collection completely sold out and her new collection *A Lope of Time* (Shoestring, March 2009) has already had to be reprinted.

Meg Peacocke has been at various times wife, mother, grandmother, teacher, counsellor and small farmer. She has an abiding passion for walking off the beaten track and for music and the visual arts. Peterloo Poets published four collections of her poems between 1998 and 2008. In 2005 she received a Cholmondeley Award.

Elisabeth Rowe read English at Oxford and worked as teacher, social worker and Advice Bureau Manager. She is married, with three children and nine grandchildren, and lives on Dartmoor. Her first collection was *Surface Tension* (Peterloo). Her poems have won prizes in many competitions and featured in several journals and anthologies.

Hermione Sandall lives in Shropshire with her husband. She started writing poetry to understand her own feelings, and then became interested in poetic form. She has two sons, has retired from drama teaching, and spends her summers sailing.

Gina Shaw lives in Ilkley. Her poems have been published in magazines and feature in other Grey Hen publications. She is a member of Second Bite, a group of three poets who give readings in the West Yorkshire area and are to perform at this year's Ilkley Literature Festival.

Pat Simmons grew up in London, but escaped as soon as she could, to Oxford and then Bristol. She was a copywriter with Oxfam and then head of communications for the African development organisation Send a Cow. Retirement has given her the chance to take her poetry writing more seriously.

Diane Tang was born in Euclid, Ohio, came to England in the 1960s as a student and more or less stayed. She worked in publishing for many years and lives in north-west London. From the early 1990s her poems have won awards and have appeared in a number of magazines.

181

Isobel Thrilling was born in Suffolk and raised in Yorkshire; she read English at Hull and worked as Head of ESL in London. She has a son, a daughter and two granddaughters. A prizewinner (Bridport and York), she has been widely published: magazines, anthologies, radio and television. Her latest book is *The Language Creatures* (Shearsman 2007).

Josie Walsh was born in Cambridge. Since her retirement from FE her poems have been published in magazines and anthologies. A Pennine poet, she has read at various venues and festivals, including Adelaide Fringe. Her first collection, *Breathing Space* (Ox Eye Press 2004), was published on completion of a Poetry MA.

Christine Webb's collection *After Babel* was published by Peterloo Poets in 2004, and she is currently completing a Creative Writing MA, studying with Jo Shapcott and Andrew Motion. In 2007 her poem 'Seven Weeks' won the *Poetry London* competition, while 'Salt' won second prize in *Mslexia*.

Pat Winslow's most recent poetry collections include *Unpredictable Geometry* and *Dreaming of Walls Repeating Themselves* (Templar Poetry). Pat's fiction has won competitions and appears in anthologies and magazines. She is currently working as a writer in residence at a prison.

Margaret Wood grew up in rural north-east Scotland and studied French and English at Aberdeen University. She now lives in Wick, where she escaped teaching to become the local registrar. She's had fiction for adults and children published in mainstream women's magazines. A college course has rekindled her interest in writing poetry.

Index of Poets

Acknowledgments

ANN ALEXANDER: 'Generation Gap' *Facing Demons* Peterloo 2002; 'The Sod It Years', 'Still It Ain't Over' and 'Listing' *Nasty, British & Short* Peterloo 2007; 'Found It' published in *Magma*. ALICE BEER: 'Encounter' *Facing Forward Looking Back* Poetry Monthly Press 1999; 'On Growing Old' and 'This Morning' *Talking of Pots, People and Points of View* poetry p f 2005. CONNIE BENSLEY: 'Last Haiku' *Choosing To Be a Swan* Bloodaxe 1994; 'Why Didn't You Tell Me You Were Dead' and 'In a Flash' *Private Pleasures* Bloodaxe 2007; 'Save Your Breath' published in *The Spectator*. PAT BORTHWICK: 'Forecast' and 'A Very Private Conversation' *Admiral Fitzroy's Barometer* Templar 2008. CAROLE BROMLEY: 'After Dad Died' published in *Mslexia*; 'Gap Year' published in *Seam*. A C CLARKE: 'Quest' published in *Envoi*; a version of 'For My Son on His Birthday' published in *Weyfarers*. CHRISTINE COLEMAN: 'First Born' published in *Writing on Water* Ragged Raven 2005; 'Legacy' published in *The White Car* Ragged Raven 2006. ANN DRYSDALE: 'Delivery from the "Crem"' and 'Feeding the Ducks at Calstock' *Between Dryden and Duffy* Peterloo 2005; 'Sleeping Together', 'Going Light' and 'Delivery from the "Crem"' *Discussing Wittgenstein* Cinnamon Press 2009. HILARY ELFICK: 'Macedoine' *The Third Mile* Guildford Poets Press 2008; 'Evensong' to be published in *Rhyme and Reason*. KATE FOLEY: 'Where's the Steeple?' *A Year Without Apricots* Backwater Press 1999; 'Thrift' *The Silver Rembrandt* Shoestring Press 2008. BERTA FREISTADT: 'To a Young Woman' *Sister-Stranger* Sidewalk Revolution 1993. JUNE HALL: 'Stile', The Shake', 'Not On Display', 'Untimely' and 'We Two' *The Now of Snow* Belgrave Press 2004. BERNIE KENNY: 'Gold is Lonely' *Isle of Thorns* 2006; 'The Blue Armchair' published in *The Launde Bag* Second Light Network 2008. ANGELA KIRBY: 'Waiting Room', 'Mr. Irresistible', 'Shacking-up Is Hard To Do' and 'The Grey-haired Woman Dead-heads Her Roses' *Mr. Irresistible* Shoestring Press 2005; 'I Have Looked on the Faces of the Dead', 'Legacies' and 'The Funeral at Langho' *Dirty Work* Shoestring Press 2008. WENDY KLEIN: 'Some Midnights' *Cuba in the Blood* Cinnamon 2009; 'If I Cannot' published in *Boomslang*. GILL LEARNER: 'Larder' read on Radio 3, St. Valentine's Day 2007; 'Becoming' published in *Envoi*. DINAH LIVINGSTONE: 'Who Are You?', 'Daughter' and 'Embodiment' *Kindness* Katabasis 2007. JANET LOVERSEED: 'Remembering a Future' published in *Equinox*. ALWYN MARRIAGE: 'By Heart' and 'Skin' *Touching Earth* Overstep 2007. GERDA MAYER: 'The Birthright' *Monkey on the Analyst's Couch* Ceolfrith Press 1980; 'Lieselott Among the Blackberries' *Hop Picker's Holiday* Happy Dragons Press 2003. GILL MCEVOY: 'Amnesty' *Uncertain Days* Happenstance Press 2006; 'Observing My Future' published in *THE SHOp*; 'Lullaby' published in *Raindog*. LYN MOIR: 'Nothing', 'Winter Love' and 'No Easy Way' *Me and Galileo* Arrowhead 2001; 'Not Exactly a David' *Breakers' Yard* Arrowhead 2003. JENNY MORRIS: 'Going Back' *Windows* Tonbridge Anthology 2007. RUTH O'CALLAGHAN: 'Entering Alzheimers' and 'Returning Veva' *Where Acid Has Etched* bluechrome 2007. M R PEACOCKE: 'Selling Up' and 'Nanny Besom' *Speaking of the Dead* Peterloo 2003; 'On the Way Down' (first published in *The London Magazine*), '"How nimble the old are"' and 'Running' *In Praise of Aunts* Peterloo 2008. ISOBEL THRILLING: 'Age' *The Ultrasonics of Snow* Riveline/Graphine 1985; 'Life Work' (as 'Reading the Runes') *The Language Creatures* Shearsman 2007. CHRISTINE WEBB: 'Dark Matter', and 'Slipping Away' *After Babel* Peterloo 2004; 'Seven Weeks' published in *Poetry London*; 'Inside the Mirror' published in Carol Ann Duffy's Poetry Corner, *Daily Mirror* 2008. PAT WINSLOW: 'Burly' *Unpredictable Geometry* Templar Poetry 2008.

Joy Howard is a co-founder of Grey Hen Press. Her poems have featured in several anthologies: *Beautiful Barbarians* (Onlywomen1987), *Dancing the Tightrope* (Women's Press 1987), *Naming the Waves* (Virago 1988), *Not for the Academy* (Onlywomen 1999) and *The Argent Moon* (Pembrokeshire Press 2007). She is a contributor to Grey Hen's first publication, *Second Bite*, which is also the name of a group of three older women poets, of which Joy is a founder member, who give readings together. She has published a collection of poems, *Exit Moonshine* (Grey Hen Press 2009) about her 'coming out' experiences in the 1980s; magazine publications include *Sofia*, *Sphinx* and *The Interpreter's House*. Shortlisted in several competitions, she was a Chapter One Open Poetry prizewinner in 2007. Her poems can be found online at *Guardian Unlimited* and *poetry p f,* and feature in 'Poems While You Wait' at St James's Hospital in Leeds. Her work has been selected for a new anthology from Headland Publications in 2009.

www.greyhenpress.com